the PLEASURE *of* *my* COMPANY

FINDING THE MOTIVATION AND COURAGE TO SPEND TIME ALONE

SUSAN MORRELL

The author can be contacted with your comments or questions at pleasuremycompany_sm@yahoo.com.

ISBN: 1-4793-2192-3
ISBN-13: 978-1-4793-2192-6
Library of Congress Control Number: 2012917395
CreateSpace, North Charleston, SC

Materials excerpted from the book **CONVERSATIONS WITH GOOD BOOK 2** © *1997 by Neale Donald Walsch* with permission from Hampton Roads Publishing c/o Red Wheel/Weiser, LLC, Newburyport, MA and San Francisco, CA www.redwheelweiser.com.

Dedication

This book is dedicated to

Frank Nyitrai & Gloria Morrell Nyitrai

whose incredible parenting instilled in me
a passion for learning,
a love for adventure
and a strong sense of self.

CONTENTS

ACKNOWLEDGEMENTS

I would be remiss if I did not acknowledge those special individuals without whose assistance I could not have published this book. First and foremost, while it goes without saying, I'm going to say it anyway–I am grateful to my family and friends for their lifelong support and encouragement of all my writing projects.

Special thanks go to my childhood friend, Barb Murray Heiss, who first put the 'bug in my ear' to compile these accounts of my life into a book. I suspect she was tired of hearing me tell the same stories over and over. "Give them a book so they can read all about it!" she would say. Well, Barb, now I can!

I extend my heartfelt appreciation to my Park City girlfriends, whose names I cannot mention here because I risk forgetting one–you know who you are!–who read this book over the summer of 2012 and gently offered me their editorial comments and genuine support.

Finally, I give thanks to the Universal Spirit that guided me to the magical mountains of Park City, Utah, for it was here that I was inspired to finally complete this book and to trust in that same Spirit to manifest its publication and distribution 'all in good time.'

PREFACE

How difficult is it for you to spend time alone? I don't mean sitting on the couch watching television or reading a magazine. I mean doing something out in public alone, without a buddy. Like going to the movies. Taking a class. Or—and this seems to be a real tough one for many people—sitting down in a restaurant to eat a full meal.

Maybe those things don't bother you. Then, how about driving alone for eight hours? Or taking a vacation by yourself? Maybe a weekend at the beach, a week at a dude ranch, a month in Great Britain. Is your heart racing just thinking about doing one of these? Do inexplicable fears keep you from even trying any of them?

Often, Life's situations or timing create alone circumstances, such as a divorce, separation or the recent death of your partner. Possibly you've moved because of a job and don't know anyone in your new city. Or perhaps you just feel the need to stretch your wings and explore new territories on your own. Many of us are apprehensive at the prospect of doing the simplest of activities without accompaniment. Women's flocking to the bathroom comes to mind! Yet, feelings of discomfort are not limited to women—men can also experience trepidations at the prospect of being alone.

Age and culture also play a role in our comfort level with doing things on our own. Some people have never spent an extended period of time alone. Many a woman, for example, went from living at home with parents and siblings to, possibly, college dorm life to marriage and family. Then the time came when the kids moved out and the marriage either ended or her spouse died and she was all alone—or I should say, Alone, with a capital A—for the first time in her life. *Now what? How do I go forward by myself?* And, yes, this same scenario has played out for men as well.

Well, I want you to know that, if just the thought of spending time in your own company makes you nervous or uncomfortable and keeps you from doing it, you're missing out on a lot of good experiences. I'm also here to say that I understand where you're coming from—I had some of the same apprehensions once. But, through a series of events, planned and unplanned by me, I have been able to overcome those fears. And, in doing so, I've met a lot of wonderful people, been to fantastic places and—perhaps, most importantly—come to know myself a lot better.

So, regardless of your reason, are you ready to explore the experience of spending time on your own? I imagine the answer to that question is 'yes' since you've picked up this book and are sitting here reading it—alone, I assume. Okay, let's begin your journey!

CHAPTER ONE

ON BEING ALONE

Allow me to clarify something right up front. I am not a hermit or a social misfit. I enjoy the company of others and often seek it out. I like spending time with family and friends. I enjoy dating interesting and fun men. You see, I don't choose to be alone out of fear of being with people. On the contrary, I've discovered that my time with others is enhanced by the time I spend alone.

There are many ways to be alone. All of us are by ourselves sometime or other during a day. Taking a shower. Driving to work or school. Shopping for groceries. Doing the laundry. Mowing the lawn. Who doesn't look forward to those moments of quiet "down time" away from the people, pressures and responsibilities of our lives, when we can kick off our shoes and grab the carpet with our toes? (Remember Bruce Willis doing this in the movie "Die Hard!") You've probably heard the expression, "feeling alone in a crowded room." Aloneness can be a physical state or a state of mind.

Why would I want to do things by myself when it's more fun with someone else? you may ask. Sure it's fun to do things with friends and I'm not suggesting you abandon them. But what about the times when no one's available? Have you ever wanted to see a movie but everyone

1

you ask to go with you is either busy or not interested in the movie you want to see? Aren't there times when you'd like to do something special—like see an art exhibit that's only in town a few days; go ice skating on a Sunday afternoon; or, spend a weekend at a spa or golf resort—but you can never find anyone who's ready or willing to go when you are? If you've foregone these types of activities just because you had no one to accompany you, you've been cheating yourself.

What I'll be addressing in the rest of the book are ways of spending time in the pleasure of your own company. I'll talk about doing things and going places alone, fun adventures away from the privacy of your home and comfort zone. But before you can get comfortable *doing* or *going*, you should understand the value of *being* alone.

What does it mean?

I'd like you to try something here. Without looking ahead in this chapter or giving it too much thought and using as few words as possible, what is your definition of the word "alone?" Don't proceed until you have one…

I typed in the word "alone" on my computer and checked the thesaurus for synonyms. The three that came up were: *unaccompanied, only* and *lonely.* I then checked each of these words for their synonyms, and here's what I discovered.

Unaccompanied also means *by yourself; on your own; single-handedly; unaided; without help. Only* also means *no one else. Lonely* also means *lonesome; abandoned; deserted; isolation; forlorn; solitary.*

That's quite a diverse range of meanings for one little word, isn't it? Which definition is similar to yours? Your answer probably reveals a lot about how you think and feel about being alone. After all, feeling that you're doing something "single-handedly" is a lot more positive than feeling "forlorn." This is an important concept to understand because, until you consider being alone a positive experience, you will continue to have difficulty doing it.

I noticed one word that was missing from these lists, a word that conveys an uplifting, peaceful meaning to alone—*solitude*. While loneliness implies loss, solitude implies peace and quiet. Solitude can benefit us in many ways. Emotionally, it provides us with a retreat away from the trials and pressures of our day-to-day lives, allowing us to resolve problems and realign ourselves, something that is difficult to do surrounded by people.

Solitude can also benefit our social lives. According to Ester Schaler Buchholz, Ph.D., professor of applied psychology at New York University's School of Education and author of *The Call of Solitude: Alonetime in a World of Attachment* (Simon & Schuster, 1997), "When you're always surrounded by people and living life in the fast lane and you don't have time to refuel, you're going to get very irritable and push people away from you. Researchers say that having time alone can actually improve your social interactions, making you a better spouse, employee and friend."

Solitude has positive effects on us physically as well. Peter Suedfeld, Ph.D., a psychologist at the University of British Columbia, in his studies of restricted environmental stimulation in lone voyages, polar stations and other solitary situations, has found that "the body's physiological response during times of solitude is similar to that of deep relaxation, especially if solitude is combined with reduced levels of sensory stimulation (e.g., the television shut off). This includes lowered heart and respiration rate, lowered blood pressure and muscle tension and reduced production of stress hormones."

Finally, solitude provides a special haven, a place where you can "hear" your inner voice and get back in touch with dreams and thoughts that are often drowned out by the outside world. Your self-esteem and self-reliance are strengthened so you can face those day-to-day situations with a higher resolve and confidence.

I would like to share with you some passages that I've read over the years that address the state of solitude or aloneness. For me, these authors have captured the values of being in a solitary state in far better words than I could hope to write.

How to Be Your Own Best Friend

The first book is one my mother sent me in a birthday "care package" when I was living in New York. The book, entitled "How to Be Your Own Best Friend," was published in 1971 and written by Mildred Newman and Bernard Berkowitz with Jean Owen. This husband-and-wife team of psychoanalysts answered questions posed to them by Ms. Owen.

These questions addressed the issues of one, *Why we, more so than any other previous generation, were not making the most of the many options available to us?* and two, *How could we begin to do this?* The book is a composite of their responses as if in a one-on-one conversation. My copy of this book is very dog-eared, has pages that have turned brown and are at risk of falling out and has passages underlined (I later discovered highlighters!) that I've often quoted in cards, letters and workshops. It was delivered on my doorstep at an introspective time in my life and had a tremendous effect on my growth over those years.

The following passage flows from the part of the "conversation" that discusses being an adult and letting go of our ties to parents and other authority figures in our lives.

As an adult, everything doesn't depend on pleasing others.
What others once did for you, you can now do for yourself...

4

You're your own man—or woman—now. But many people will not realize that...It's actually a childlike sense of security we're holding on to. As long as we feel small and helpless, we feel we're in the presence of invisible, all-powerful adults...To be abandoned is a terrifying prospect to a child; he literally couldn't survive it. But for an adult, aloneness is something quite different. He not only can survive, he often needs aloneness to grow, to get to know himself and develop his powers. Someone who cannot tolerate aloneness is someone who doesn't know he's grown up.

It takes courage to let go of that fantasy of childhood safety. The world may never seem so certain again, but what fresh air we breathe when we take possession of our own separateness, our own integrity! That's when our adult life really begins. (Newman & Berkowitz 54-57)

My adult life, at least in the sense of letting go of safety nets, began the spring of 1975, six months after receiving that book. I was living in Westchester County, New York, and working for Xerox Corporation. In February of '75, I visited a friend in Tucson, Arizona, and fell in love with the area. On my return, I called another friend who had worked with me in New York, but who had moved to Phoenix when her husband was transferred. I wanted to know if there were any openings at the Xerox branch there because I wanted to transfer to Arizona.

As luck would have it, she was pregnant with twins and, on her doctor's orders, had just given her notice. Her boss talked to my boss, I interviewed over the phone and I got her job! In May, I packed up my things, dropped them off at my family's house in Ohio (along with my car) and flew to Phoenix. Once there, I rented a car and a kitchenette room at a hotel near the office and began my new job.

I found a furnished apartment a few weeks later, and my sister and her fiancé drove my car and possessions out. By June, I was an official resident of Phoenix, Arizona.

Talk about being alone! I knew absolutely no one in Phoenix, with the exception of Alison, who, as a new mom, was decidedly living a different lifestyle than me at this point. Unlike living in New York, I could no longer drive home for a quick weekend visit whenever I felt like it. I was hundreds—no, thousands—of miles from all my friends and family. Was I lonely? Sure, at times. But mostly, I thrived!

I call my year in Phoenix my "metamorphosis period," which seemed very appropriate seeing as I was living in the city named for the mythical bird that rose from its own ashes to be born anew. I really got to "...know [myself] and develop [my] powers" to paraphrase Newman and Berkowitz.

That summer, at the age of 25, I learned how to swim—something I'd feared since childhood. Being born under the astrological water sign of Scorpio, one might expect that I'd love the water. Instead, it caused me untold anxiety. My parents enrolled me in swimming lessons, to no avail. You see, I was very shy as a child, and those group classes intimidated me because of the other students and because of having to display my inadequacies. Not that I expressed it in those terms back then, of course. Instead, I acted it out by crying or arguing or pleading in order to avoid that trip to the YWCA. Eventually, my parents relented.

While I greatly appreciated their actions at the time, as I got older I sometimes wished they'd been a little firmer with me. Like when a summer social event would leave me sitting on the sidelines while my friends were cavorting in the pool. I think my fear of swimming centered on the "deep end," the waters over my head. I can relate this back to an incident that happened at a family outing when I was about ten.

My family spent a week in Canada visiting my uncle's family who had rented a cabin up there for the summer. There was a small lake, of course, and a wooden platform quite a distance from the shore. Folks could swim or row out there and spend the day jumping into the lake or lying on towels to catch the sun's rays. Somehow, they managed to convince me that if I went out in the rowboat, I could enjoy myself playing on the platform—I wouldn't have to go in the water at all.

Well, once there, my uncle decides to convince me how much fun being in the water can be—he threw me in and jumped in after me to make sure I was all right. Needless to say, I wasn't! I panicked and thrashed and screamed! Slimy plant life wrapped itself around my legs and freaked me out. I lost my flip-flops. It was awful! They got me back on the platform in what seemed like hours, but was really a matter of minutes. My father gave his brother hell for what he'd done, and my uncle apologized to me. But that memory stays with me to this day. (And I still only swim in clear, chlorinated swimming pools, leaving the natural bodies of water for the little fishies and slimy plants!)

Anyway, that summer in Phoenix I decided to learn to swim. As I walked out of the locker room to the outside pool (Yes, the pool was outdoors—it was August in Arizona, after all!), my blood pressure rose, my stomach did somersaults and my mind kept asking, "*Do I really want to do this?*" There were six women in my class, and the instructor was an eighteen-year old Adonis named Matt. He had us enter the water off the edge in the shallow end and then introduce ourselves to the group. So far, so good!

I soon realized that my fear was minimal compared to another's. There was a woman in the group who was absolutely terrified of being in the water—shallow or otherwise. She hung onto the side of the pool as if her life depended on it—and I'm sure in her mind it did. I used this information to motivate myself—I'm not as bad off as I thought! Perhaps there's hope for me after all! Six weeks later, I was diving off the low board in the deep end, swimming the length of the Olympic-sized pool and passing my test. It took me over twenty years, but I'd finally learned to swim. I learned something else that summer, though, something of even more value. I learned how to overcome my fears by trusting others, trusting in my own powers of accomplishment and taking that all-important first step.

Another new adventure for me was joining the Sierra Club. I'd fallen in love with the desert—it was so different from the Midwest and the East. So beautiful in its starkness, powerful in its simplicity, breathtaking in its vastness. As a member of the club, we hiked the Superstition, Camelback and Squaw Peak Mountains surrounding Phoenix. I remember one tour guide, a woman who reminded me of Mammy Yokum from the Li'l Abner comic strip, corncob pipe and all. She was of questionable age, her skin permanently tanned and dried by the desert sun, her eyes wrinkled but shiny and alert. But, despite her diminutive size and advanced years, it was a challenge to keep up with her as we traversed the rocky trails and crossed the crusty earth of the Superstition Mountains.

I came to love hiking. Some weekend mornings, I would get up before dawn and hike Squaw Peak, go off the trail at a favorite spot and sit facing east to watch the sun rise above the valley. I felt closer to my soul, to God, in that venue than I'd ever felt anywhere before in my life!

It seems only natural then that, while getting in touch with my soul through nature, I would explore my spiritual self through a new phenomenon–Transcendental Meditation. It was being introduced to the Western world by a soft-spoken man with a head of wiry gray hair and beard, garbed in a white sheet-like garment and sandals, known as the Mahareshi Mahesh Yogi.

After seeing the Mahareshi on the Merv Griffin television show, I attended a local lecture on TM and decided to learn how to do it. It was a simple, private first lesson as my sponsor guided me through the process. He whispered my mantra into my ear, and it has become a silent sound inside my soul, never spoken except by my mind's voice when I meditate. TM was a monumental life-shifting experience and precursor to further spiritual development in the years since.

I had no idea when I decided to move to Arizona that I would undergo such a transformation. I was clearly an independent woman who had truly grown up and taken "…possession of [her] own separateness, [her] own integrity." I had become my own best friend!

Gift from the Sea

The next book was originally published in 1955 and later updated by the author in 1975. "Gift from the Sea" was written by Anne Morrow Lindbergh, wife of pilot Charles Lindbergh. This simple, yet profound, book is a study of the stages of a woman's life as compared to seashells that Ms. Lindbergh found during a vacation alone on an island. In Chapter three, entitled "Moon Shell," she reflects on solitude while studying the single, central point of this shell's spiraling design.

We are all, in the last analysis, alone. And this basic state of solitude is not something we have any choice about. It is, as the poet Rilke says, "not something that one can take or leave. We

9

are solitary. We may delude ourselves and act as though this were not so. That is all. But how much better it is to realize that we are so, yes, even to begin by assuming it. Naturally," he goes on to say, "we will turn giddy."

Naturally. How one hates to think of oneself as alone. How one avoids it. It seems to imply rejection or unpopularity. An early wallflower panic still clings to the word. One will be left, one fears, sitting in a straight-backed chair alone, while the popular girls are already chosen and spinning around the dance floor with their hot-palmed partners. We seem so frightened today of being alone that we never let it happen. Even if family, friends and movies should fail, there is still the radio or television to fill up the void…we choke the space with continuous music, chatter and companionship to which we do not even listen. It is simply there to fill the vacuum. When the noise stops there is no inner music to take its place. We must re-learn to be alone. (Lindbergh 41-42)

When you get in your car, do you immediately turn on the radio or pop in a CD? At work, do you have to have a radio playing softly in the background while you perform your tasks? When you get home from work, do you turn on the television or put on some music while you go about changing clothes, doing chores or preparing dinner? If you're home all day with children or waiting for them to return from school, must you have other sounds in the house besides your child's laughter or the vacuum's drone? Has your smart phone become permanently attached to your hand so that in a free moment you're automatically texting or tweeting someone?

I know all of these to be true in one way or another for family members and friends. And I'm not here to say there's anything wrong with any of them. Living alone, even I enjoy the "company" of voices coming from the television while I'm in the kitchen chopping onions or stirring pasta in the pot. What I want to address is how *unconsciously* these things are done in order to *"choke the space with continuous music, chatter and companionship to which we do not even listen."* What is it about that space that frightens us so much that we need to fill it?

Somehow, sometime in my adult life, without consciously trying to cultivate this habit, I learned to be in the silence. I almost never have the radio on in my car, preferring to drive in silence than have my auditory senses attacked by the noise of disc jockeys, commercials and music that doesn't strike a chord with me at that moment. If I do want to hear music, I'd much rather put in a CD and listen to the kind of music that matches my particular mood and not have it interrupted by commercials and chatter.

But, more often, there's no sound emanating from my car speakers. Instead, I find driving to be a time of observation and contemplation. As it happens, many of my major life decisions or ideas have come to me while driving. It's a perfect opportunity for self-talk, for working through your thoughts about a problem, a decision that has to be made or a paper that has to be written. For instance, when I was taking a poetry class at university in the early '90s, I started keeping a hand-held tape recorder in the console in my car. As lines for poems I had to write for class would come to mind in the quiet of my drives, I'd record them and transcribe the tape later. I didn't want to risk losing the thought. More significantly, by driving in the silence, I was able to "hear" the thought, such as the one that prompted this poem, which later won me a third-place award in the Midwest Writers' Conference in Canton, Ohio:

Oreo Cookies

I eat Oreo cookies whole and complete.
I don't twist them apart.
I don't lick the cream filling
then eat the chocolate wafers.
I eat Oreo cookies whole and complete.

I don't drink milk.
It can flavor my coffee,
soften my cereal,
and fluff my mashed potatoes,
but I don't drink milk.

I *do* dunk my Oreos in milk.
I plunge the cookie in the glass,
my thumb and forefinger skimming the surface,
as tiny brown flecks speckle
the opaque white liquid.

Dunking an Oreo is an art.
Retrieve too soon, and it's too hard.
Submerge too long and—plop!
I test it with a pinch: gooey on the outside,
yet firm in the center.

Placing the morsel upon my tongue
like a communion wafer, I close my mouth.
No chewing. No biting.
I just savor the feel of it
between my tongue and palate.

Cocoa and lactose scents caress my nostrils.
Mushy pulp oozes around my teeth.
My mouth salivates,
my jaw gyrates,
and my tongue licks my lips.

The Oreo cookie,
still whole but transformed,
dissolves
and fills me with delight.

If you want to love me,
love me like an Oreo cookie—
whole and complete.
Don't twist me apart.
Don't dissect me,
keeping what you like
and trying to change the rest.

Love all of me.
Love the hard and soft of me.
Love the in and out of me.
Taste me. Savor me.
Delight in me.

Then, if you want to love me,
if you want to be
the milk that melts my heart,
I'll submerse myself in you—
wholly and completely—
like an Oreo cookie.

In the preface of this book, I asked you to imagine driving alone for eight hours. Well, I've made those drives countless times, many of them when I lived in Westchester County, New York, and Chicago, Illinois, and I would travel back to northeast Ohio to visit my family. More to the point, I've been known to make those long drives *without ever touching my radio dial or popping in a tape.* Hard for you to imagine? Actually, that's unusual for me, too, since I always had my case of tapes with me for those long trips. I couldn't believe it, though, when I realized I'd driven seven hours–from Bedford Hills, New York, to the Mercer exit on Route 80 in western Pennsylvania–without listening to one note of music! Now, I'm not saying this kind of solitude is right for everyone. But I would challenge you to experience it once in a while and see where it takes you and what you discover about yourself on the journey.

Conversations with God

The final book is one I've read more recently. I think the passage can touch everyone's heart, regardless of spiritual beliefs or religious affiliations. It can be found in "Conversations with God, Book 2" by Neale Donald Walsch.

> *When was the last time you sat alone with the silence, traveling to the deepest part of your being? When was the last time you said hello to your soul? (Walsch 100)*

I just love that phrase, saying "hello to your soul." This is the ultimate expression of self-talk, of getting in touch with that part of you where all your thoughts and ideas originate. I think of it as visiting my wellspring and drawing on the "waters" that nourish my entire being–body, mind and soul. I firmly believe in the power of our personal spirits and of the universal Spirit that flows through us all. There are so many names for this force and so many beliefs built around our many concepts of it. My intent here is not to expound on, or preach about, my beliefs. Rather, I offer this quote as a suggestion for you to get in touch with your own beliefs by going to that ultimate place of aloneness–to the solitude of your soul.

Electronic Solitude

I'd be remiss if I didn't acknowledge a new form of aloneness that society has embraced, one that I'll call 'electronic solitude.' In this age of smart phones, MP3 players, handheld movie screens and video games, we've created invisible walls around ourselves as we focus on those miniature apparatuses that have become appendages to our bodies.

But this is not true 'alone' time. Social media, in my opinion, are isolating us in ways that are detrimental to our need for solitude, not beneficial. The value of spending time alone comes from the introspection that we experience, both consciously and unconsciously, while in those moments of solitary activity. However, solitary activity is *not* about shutting people out to the point of disconnecting from them. It's not about being rude by allowing an electronic device to interrupt or distract from one's interaction with others. It's not about tuning out the world only to become lost in a false world of texts, trends and tweets.

The *value* of alone time is directly proportionate to the amount of time you are willing to devote to consciously spending time in your own company. The value increases as your self-awareness and self-confidence increase. The value is how empowered you feel when you recognize and accept *your* value—as a human being and as a spiritual being.

Chapter One - Recommendations

1. How do you "choke the space" you live in? Select one of the ways you do this. Then, for a week (or whatever period of time you want to designate), change that behavior and allow yourself to just be in the vacuum. If it helps, keep a journal of your experiences during this time. What effect does this new behavior have on you physically? Mentally? Emotionally? What have you discovered about yourself? Did you hear any "inner music?" When ready, try another behavior to change and see how the experiences differ or are similar.

2. Keep a log for a month (to allow patterns to emerge) of the time you consciously spend being alone, doing things that are already part of your lifestyle as well as adding new "alone" things to your routine. For each event, make note of:
    a. Day of the week
    b. Time of day
    c. Length of time spent (even five minutes of conscious alone time counts)
    d. The "alone" action: driving in silence, shooting hoops, walking, visiting a museum, playing golf, etc.
    e. Degree of safety you experienced:
        1 = Very anxious
        2 = Mostly anxious, but some comfort
        3 = Equally anxious and comfortable
        4 = Mostly comfortable, but some anxiety
        5 = Very comfortable

    Do you see any patterns emerging? What kinds of activities are more comfortable than others? Why do you think that is? What surprises did you find?

3. Say "hello" to your soul. In whatever way most suits you, make a conscious effort throughout the day to do this. It can be as simple as closing your eyes for a moment or two at a red light; while using the computer; or, while waiting in line somewhere. It can take the form of a prayer or meditation. Simply say the words in your mind–"hello, soul." There is no right or wrong way–just *your* way.

Suggestions

1. "Gift from the Sea" by Anne Morrow Lindbergh

2. "How to Be Your Own Best Friend" by Mildred Newman and Bernard Berkowitz with Jean Owen

3. The "Conversations with God" series of books by Neale Donald Walsch

4. "Illusions: The Adventures of a Reluctant Messiah." 1977. Richard Bach. Delacorte Press. New York, New York. I particularly like the parable within the parable at the beginning of this book about a clinging water creature who lets go and travels down the stream alone. The main story tells of the "author's" encounter with a man who, though knowing himself to be a messiah, is reluctant to live that life and to experience the loneliness that comes with the territory.

5. "Wisdom of the Ages" by Dr. Wayne Dyer. This is a great book for those quiet moments of solitude. Dr. Dyer has compiled

sixty of his favorite passages written by a variety of people throughout the ages, people he describes as teachers, such as, Pythagoras, Omar Khayyam, Jesus of Nazareth, Henry David Thoreau, e.e. cummings and Martin Luther King, Jr. The topics covered include patience, triumph, being childlike, enthusiasm, solitude, individuality, appreciation and more. The short chapters lend themselves to a quick read or to a longer period of contemplation, depending on your mood.

CHAPTER TWO

PLAYING BY YOURSELF

A s I prepared to write this book, I looked back on my life to see if there were any patterns that could define my eventual interest in spending time by myself—or, as author Iyanla Vanzant likes to refer to it, being *with* myself. If you're thinking perhaps I was an only child, you're wrong. I was, however, the first born child of Frank and Gloria Nyitrai *and* the first grandchild born to both sides of the family. So, for two and a half years—until the arrival of my cousin, Danny, and my sister, Sandy—I was the only child in two families. Not that I was aware of this unique position. But I'm sure it had some effect on my psyche and helped to create the need in me to get away from the crowd and be on my own.

Some would cite my birth order as an important factor in my development, and I'm sure it has a lot to do with who I am. For over ten years, there was just my sister and me in my immediate family. Sandy was a typical second child in that she was much more sociable than I, having hordes of friends in both of the neighborhoods in which we grew up. She was part of a group, while I played with my selected favorites or alone.

One memory that comes to mind is when we lived next door to my maternal grandparents. This was when I was four to ten years old. Both Cape Cod houses had patios in the back that became my havens. I would pretend that our patio was the downstairs of my "house" and theirs was the upstairs, and the driveway between was my "staircase." Or, if I was feeling adventurous, our patio was my command center and theirs was the enemy's fortress to be broken into. I wasn't always alone when playing between these two "stages," but I was alone often enough that I distinctly remember those times. With fondness, I might add.

When I was ten years old, we moved two streets away to a brand new house. In fact, we were one of the first families to move into the new development. The street was what we called a "double dead end"—one end curved and ended at a woods and the other stopped at an Ohio Edison power station. Access to the street was from two side roads that ended at our street. So, there wasn't any through traffic, which afforded us kids the benefit of the street as a playground. The manhole cover in front of our driveway was home plate in many a game of kick ball. There was talk of continuing the road through the woods someday, but fortunately that never happened. Today, it's still the same quiet neighborhood it was when we moved there in 1959.

Anyway, as luck would have it, most of the kids who moved into the neighborhood were Sandy's age, and she quickly had her new group of friends. I, on the other hand, had a girl three years older than me who lived across the street. That first summer, we hung out together, playing with Barbie dolls and climbing around the dirt piles in the lots still being developed. But, she and I never really clicked. Being three years older than me, she matured a lot faster than I did and was soon more interested in what all teenage girls are interested in—

other teenage girls and, of course, boys. Definitely not in a ten-year-old hanger-on. And, truth be told, I wasn't particularly interested in her either. So, I found myself being driven to girlfriends' homes to spend time, entertaining them at my house or playing by myself.

Treasures and sleuthing

Now, I don't want to mislead you here. I also played with my sister and the other kids on the street. I wasn't antisocial, after all. I was a kid who liked to do what most kids liked to do who grew up in the Sixties. When indoors, my sister and I played together. Monopoly on Saturday mornings was a favorite. In fact, any board game could keep us busy for hours. Then, there was the clue game we made up. Each of us would take a room in the house and hide a small "treasure" for the other to find. We'd write clues in the form of riddles and hide them throughout the room, eventually leading to the treasure. Handing off clue number one, we'd race to see who could find the other's treasure first. This treasure could be a piece of jewelry, a small bank, a figurine–whatever we fancied. Depending on our moods and the time we had, we'd decide on a ten-, fifteen- or twenty-clue game. What fun we had!

The point I want to make, though, is that I could just as easily entertain myself and, contrary to my sister, often preferred to do that. Sometimes, I'd put on my roller skates—the metal kind that you put on over your shoes and used a key to tighten until your pinky toes were crying out in pain—and I'd skate around the basement floor to Grieg's "In the Hall of the Mountain King" from the Peer Gynt Suite. Arms swinging from side to side like pendulums in front of my body, I'd increase my speed as the metal wheels clacked over the cold, cement floor. Sometimes, I'd grab a gray support pole and swirl around and around it, my head tilted back, my hair flying out behind me. The gradually-increasing tempo and cymbal-crashing finale made for an exhilarating skating session. (Unfortunately, this came to an end when my parents laid carpeting and furnished most of the basement for entertaining friends.)

At the age of eleven, my mom introduced me to Nancy Drew, giving me three of her own Nancy Drew books that she'd saved to pass on to her daughter someday. I soon had a new "best friend," and one of my favorite "alone" things to do was read my Nancy Drew books. Going into my bedroom and closing the door, though, did not afford me enough of the privacy I wanted when getting lost in one of Nancy's mysteries. So, I set up my closet as a sort-of library. I had one of those long, narrow, sliding-door closets. I lined my Nancy Drew books on the floor, hung a flashlight from a belt between my clothes and put some well-placed pillows on the floor and against the wall.

Then, sliding shut the door, I'd seclude myself for hours reading. Sometimes I'd put a glass of water and a Hershey bar outside the door (there wasn't enough room inside) and I'd open the door to get a bite or a sip. Before I knew it—and often long before I'd take notice—my derriere would get numb and my legs would get cramped. But that didn't deter me. Nancy and I were comrades, you see. Her independent nature appealed to me, and I believe that a lot of who and what I am today is because of the time I spent with her, imagining myself in the role of girl detective.

And then there were three

When I was thirteen, my brother, Tony, was born. Despite the age difference, having him to play with was a delight that allowed Sandy and me to be kids again during our teenage years. Just ask him about the time we made him and his friend, Nicky, go to see the Walt Disney movie, "The Lady and the Tramp." We insisted that we were going for their benefit, when, in truth, we were using them as a reason to go ourselves. The only drawback to Tony's arrival was that Sandy and I had to once again share a bedroom, something we had done at our old house and had looked forward to *not* doing again. Gone were my closet sessions with Nancy Drew. Gone was the privacy of my own room. I found myself spending my alone time in the basement, curled up on the sofa, listening to the Beach Boys and Herman's Hermits while reading or studying.

So, you see, I come by my ability to be alone naturally. I didn't, however, sustain that ability into my adulthood for some reason. Many of my adult adventures alone required forethought and self-talk on my part before I could do them. But I'll get into that later.

Now, you may be saying, *"That's all well and good for you. But what about me? What does this have to do with my learning to be alone?"* The reason I shared these anecdotes with you is so you can see how they influenced who I am today. What I want you to do is think about your childhood. Think about the way you spent time as a child and about your place in the order of children in your immediate and extended families.

I have written some questions for you to answer about yourself, questions that will assist you with this journey down memory lane. Obviously, there are no right or wrong answers. Nor are you limited to these questions. Let your mind direct you in what you need to discover. This is an opportunity for you to get reacquainted with the child that you were and to see how that child is influencing the person you are today. Take the time to really think about your answers. Make note not just of the *facts* about your experiences, but also of your *feelings* about them. Proceed at your own pace. This is, after all, your journey—enjoy it!

Chapter Two - Recommendations

Birth Order

1. What effect has your birth order had on your life? Are you a "typical" first born? Middle child? "Baby" of the family?
2. Think about the roles you and your siblings played as children. Were you a leader or a follower? An originator or a doer? The instigator or the peacemaker? Did these roles shift and why?
3. How did you take up sides? Were the same one(s) always against the other(s)? Or did you change sides? Why or when? Were you ever the "odd man out?"

Only Child

1. If you are an only child, how did this affect you?
2. Did you create imaginary siblings to play with?
3. Were you close to a cousin as if he or she were a brother or sister?
4. Think about the role you played when interacting with other children. Were you a leader or a follower? The originator or the doer? The instigator or the peacemaker?

Alone Times

1. Recall times when you played alone. What kinds of activities could occupy your time for extended periods? Arts and crafts? Reading? Action play?
2. Did you have imaginary friends? How did you interact with them? What roles did you play?
3. What is your favorite memory of time spent alone as a child? How did you feel while in those moments? Do you still do that activity—or something similar—as an adult?

Suggestions

1. Read books on birth order and sibling placement.

2. Read (or re-read) "Little Women" by Louisa May Alcott. This is a great study in sibling roles and one of my personal favorites.

3. Discuss your observations on sibling roles with your own siblings (or with whomever you feel that kind of bond). Where do you agree and disagree? Why?

4. Buy a favorite childhood toy or activity—jacks, soldiers, a coloring book and crayons. Whatever! Now, play with them in the privacy of your home. Feel silly? That's okay. Aren't children permitted to be silly? Play with the child in you and see what you discover.

5. After doing Step 4, transfer that alone activity to a similar adult activity, one in which you can "play" and discover new interests. For example, buy some art supplies and paint or draw a picture. Teach yourself how to play chess. Go fly a kite! Don't worry about being "good" at whatever it is—the idea is just to experience it and enjoy the time with yourself.

CHAPTER THREE

ONE TICKET FOR...

Maybe now you have some idea where your attitudes about being alone originated. The interesting thing is that as adults we sometimes harbor fears about things that didn't seem to bother us as children. What comes to mind for me is riding a Ferris wheel. It was one of the first rides I'd run to at the amusement parks. With my dad sitting between my sister and me, we began our backward ascent, and I was thrilled as we made our way around and around the wheel. Today, you'd have a difficult time convincing me I should embark on a ride on one. I've even tried those new larger wheels with enclosed cages, thinking I'd feel safer. Forget it! I ended up staring at my friend's shoes the entire time.

The point I want to make is that maybe there was a time you enjoyed spending time alone, but now you don't. Why is that? How come you're so anxious about going places or doing things by yourself now? Have you become more self-conscious as you've gotten older? Are you afraid of being alone with your own thoughts? Whatever the reason, what's important now is that you are willing to face those anxieties and move beyond them.

When I examined my "alone" experiences during my adulthood, I realized that, without planning it, my experiences had started out small and progressed to the long-term trips I take today. So I'm going to start you off "small" as well—you're going to the movies alone! I have to admit that this took a bit of self-talk on my part the first time I did it. I mean, going to a movie is a date thing, right? Or something you do with a group of friends, or as an outing with the kids. But alone? How conspicuous can you get?

My first time was in 1981 while I was working for Xerox Corporation in Greenwich, Connecticut, and traveling the northeast region as a trainer. I was staying at a hotel in the Boston suburbs for several nights while training at the local branch. By the third night, I was bored with shopping, reading and watching television. Yet, when the idea to go see a movie crossed my mind, I almost laughed out loud. But the idea hung on tenaciously and the self-talk persisted, sounding something like this:

Mind:	*What's wrong with going to a movie?*
Me:	What's wrong? What will people think if I go in alone?
Mind:	*What people?*
Me:	Whoever's at the theater—the ticket seller, the food vendor, the ticket taker, people in line, people sitting around me!
Mind:	*Do you know any of these people?*
Me:	Well, no, but—
Mind:	*But, what?*
Me:	They'll wonder why I'm alone, why I don't have a date or someone else with me. Or they'll think I'm this pathetic woman because I have to go out by myself— or, worse yet, that I'm some kind of pervert!

Mind:	*Are any of those things true?*
Me:	Of course not!
Mind:	*Is that what you think of a woman when you see her alone?*
Me:	Well, I can't help but wonder why she is alone, unless—
Mind:	*Unless what?*
Me:	Unless maybe I'd envy her a little because she has the nerve to actually go to a movie by herself.
Mind:	*So, you probably wouldn't think she was a pervert?*
Me:	Of course not!
Mind:	*And even if you did, do you think she'd care?*
Me:	Probably not.
Mind:	*Then, what does it matter what a bunch of strangers whom you'll never see again thinks of you? Are you going to let them cheat you out of seeing a movie? Out of doing what you want to do?*
Me:	Well, no, I guess not.
Mind:	*So, do you want to sit in this stuffy hotel room all night or go to a movie?*
Me:	Go to a movie!
Mind:	*Then do it!*
Me:	I will!

Once I got past that initial conversation with myself, I had to decide on a movie. Unfortunately, there wasn't much playing that I really wanted to see. But, having psyched myself up for the experience, I felt I had to go through with it or lose my nerve altogether. It was a matter of principle, something I had to prove to myself that I could do. So, I decided on "War Games" with Matthew Broderick, Ally Sheedy and Dabney Coleman. A real "no brainer." A non-tearjerker. The perfect choice.

From then on, I had what I can only describe as an "in body" experience. On the outside, this cool, collected woman parked her car outside the theater; waited in line to buy one ticket; ordered one Pepsi and one bag of popcorn (Something I rarely do when I go to the movies, but I guess I needed to blend in with the crowd this time.); exchanged her one ticket for a torn stub; walked into the darkened theater; and, sat in a left-section seat about a quarter of the way down the aisle.

Inside, however, my nerves surged like live electrical wires! I was aware of everything that was going on around me. On one hand, I was sure that everything I feared would actually happen as I made my way to my seat. I was sure that all eyes were on me! I was sure I heard someone say, *"Look at her, all alone. How pathetic!"* On the other hand, I told myself, *"What makes me think they're noticing me? And who cares if they are!"*

Five minutes later, the lights went down, the film began and I was doing it. I was watching a movie in a theater all alone! And, incredibly, I lived to tell about it with my reputation in tact! How about that? To this day, whenever I see the movie, "War Games," on television, I can't help but smile to myself as I remember the experience and how proud I felt while driving back to the hotel that night.

So, what did you learn from my story about taking this first small step by yourself? In my case, I had the advantage of being in a place where I knew absolutely no one, so I didn't fear running into someone to whom I'd have to explain myself. Would that make a difference to you? Then go to a theater that's not near where you live, where you're not likely to run into acquaintances.

Another advantage for me was that I attended the movie in the middle of the week, avoiding a date night when I might feel out of place among couples. If that bothers you, then go during the week.

Or to a weekend matinee. There are ways around those external excuses for *not* going to a movie alone.

Think about this. Why do we have to have someone with us during a movie? I mean, sometimes we just want to get out of the house and aren't looking for all that social stuff that goes with a date or group trip to the movies, right? So, why don't we? If there's a particular movie that we really want to see but no one else we know is interested in seeing it, why should we be deprived of it? When you think about it, we're really watching a movie alone even when we do go with someone else, aren't we? We can't talk to anyone without disturbing those around us or chance missing some of the show. So, who needs them? Go it alone! And do whatever it takes to make the experience an easy, yet memorable, one.

Chapter Three - Recommendations

1. Hold a conversation with yourself—self-talk—about why you should or shouldn't go to a movie alone. Talk out loud if that helps (preferably in the privacy of your room or car!). What reasons crop up? What excuses? What anxieties? How do they manifest themselves in you—butterflies in your stomach? Sweaty palms? Giddiness? Excitement? Dread?

2. If you've already gone to a movie alone, think about your first time. How did you feel? What was your self-talk about? Have you gone again since? If not, ask yourself *why* not and do step 1. However, if this has become a regular event for you, try this the next time you go. See if there's anyone else in the theater that's all alone. Observe how the person behaves and try to decide if this is a "first timer." Maybe a smile or a word of encouragement from you will ease this person's dis-ease. If nothing else, you'll feel good knowing how far you've come that a trip to the movies alone is no longer a traumatic event. And remembering what you learned from your first experience will help you tackle some of the other experiences later in this book.

3. Never soloed to the movies? Make a movie date with yourself! Decide on a day and time when you'll feel comfortable going. Decide on the movie theater. Then, select the movie. Or, if you really want to see a particular movie, find out where it's playing and go there. Write the date on your calendar. If it helps, think about what you'll wear. Anything that will help you prepare for this date with yourself.

4. Go to the movies! Have an "in body" experience, being aware of what's going on outside and, more importantly, *inside* of you. What are your feelings? What are your thoughts? How do you feel physically? Then, when the lights go down, settle back in your seat and enjoy the show!

5. Afterwards, give yourself a big pat on the back—I mean that literally! You deserve it! In your car—you'd better roll up the windows for this one–yell out proudly, *"Yes! I did it!"*

6. Was it good for you? If so, great! Now, keep it up. If it wasn't so good for you, that's great, too! Give yourself credit for doing something that took a lot of courage. Though I'm trying to keep this narrative lighthearted, I know that it's not as easy as it sounds, is it? Think about why it wasn't a good experience for you and make some changes in your planning. A different day or time. A different theater or seat. A different kind of movie that draws a different type of crowd. Whatever will work for you is appropriate. It's *your* experience!

CHAPTER FOUR

TABLE FOR ONE

There was an episode in the fourth season of the television show, *Frasier*, called "Odd Man Out" in which Frasier Crane goes to a posh restaurant alone for dinner. Plans to go with his producer, Roz, for her birthday fall through, as do taking his brother, Niles, or his father. And so, almost on a dare, he decides to go it alone.

From the time he enters the restaurant and throughout the course of the meal, he experiences all of the discomforts that one would imagine associated with eating out alone, albeit exaggerated. The maître d' makes a big deal of his coming alone, then of seating him at a table out in the open because it's the only one convenient for one person. The waiter noisily removes the extra place settings—clink, clink, clink of the glass and silverware—and apologizes to Frasier for the noise. Frasier replies, for the benefit of all around him, "Just because I'm alone, doesn't mean I'm lonely!" The waiter then draws even more attention to the table by calling out for a bus boy to light the candle.

Frasier tries to act nonchalant and nonplussed by the events, but it's obvious that he's self-conscious and sensitive to the people around him. He's convinced that they are all wondering about his solitary state and feeling sorry for him. To compensate, he makes convoluted attempts to explain his situation, saying out loud how much he enjoys being out alone for a change. Of course, this draws more attention to him and results in even more hilarious antics. He finally succumbs to the discomfort and joins a family who invite him to their table. The final straw is when they bring out a birthday cake he'd ordered for Roz and neglected to cancel. All in all, it was a comically traumatic experience for poor Frasier.

Fortunately, that was fiction. Your experience dining out alone need not be comical nor traumatic. Instead, it can be quite enjoyable. However, I won't kid you—for some of you this could be very difficult. Your feelings of self-consciousness may be more pronounced than when going to the movies alone. Why? Well, you won't have the darkened theater to "hide" in for one. Also, there won't be a movie distracting the other diners. You'll be right out there for all to see in your solitary splendor! Now, I don't tell you this to scare you off. I just want you to be aware of the possibility up front so you can psyche yourself up for it.

Perhaps the question that comes to mind is why would anyone want to dine out alone? Well, there are any number of occasions when this could occur—during a day of shopping; traveling out of town on business; taking a trip by yourself; or, after going to a movie alone. These are when I usually find myself dining alone, although I have occasionally gone to lunch or dinner by myself instead of cooking at home just because, at the last minute, I had a craving for a particular meal from a favorite restaurant and no one else was immediately available to go with me. Whatever the reason, consider it one more way of spending time with yourself and treating yourself to something special.

I tried to recall where and when I dined out alone for the first time, but it was so long ago that I couldn't remember the exact incident. It was most likely during a business trip while traveling the northeast states as a trainer. Remember my movie experience while staying in Boston? By then—the early '80s—I was going alone to the hotel restaurant or to local establishments for dinner after a long day at a training session.

I did my share of room service, but one can only take so much of that. It sounds elegant, but gets old after a while and is very limiting in its choices. Rarely do you find a good pasta dish on the menu, and never have I found a hotel that served fried dumplings and General Tso's chicken. You've got to go to the source for good ethnic foods. A greasy burger tastes a lot better when sitting in a booth at the local bar and grill then served up on a tray with expertly folded linens and condiments in glass bowls. I'm talking ambience here! The right atmosphere! Getting in the right frame of mind is as important for a good meal as the food.

One trick that I'll share with you if you feel the need for a little companionship while dining out alone–go to a restaurant with a bar and eat there. Seriously! Consider the bartender your "dinner companion"—he or she is a natural when it comes to chit-chat, but you'll also be left alone most of the time during the experience. You may not feel as conspicuous sitting alone at the bar as you do at an open table or booth for one. In fact, I met my husband—ex-husband now—while having dinner alone at a bar in Edinburgh, Scotland. I'll be telling you more about that trip later, but I will share with you how we met.

It was September of '83. I had arrived in Great Britain the day before and only arrived in Edinburgh that afternoon. That evening, I had tickets for the Military Tattoo, a bands-and-military-drills show held on the grounds of the Edinburgh Castle during the annual International Arts Festival. Anyway, I wanted to have dinner before the show. I was walking around downtown and had entered a couple of restaurants, but didn't get the right "feeling" from those places—too crowded, too noisy, too whatever. As I was waiting at a crosswalk for the light to change, I glanced to my left and decided to head in a different direction. I took another left and there it was—The Blithe Spirit. The name on the awning called out to me, so I ventured in.

It was a very small establishment with perhaps a dozen tables and only five seats at the tiny bar. Following my own rule, I took one of the five stools and asked the bartender for a menu. There was just one other person at the bar, sitting at the opposite end where the bar curved. He and the bartender were conversing while I read the menu, though I was half listening to them as well. Not that I could understand much, but I absolutely loved their thick Scottish accents! (To this day, the male Scottish accent is my favorite and makes me weak in the knees!) I asked the bartender what he recommended—are you ready for this? A baked potato with coleslaw and cheese topping! In fact, they had a whole list of unusual toppings for the potatoes, which were a house specialty and so big they were a meal in themselves.

As it turned out, I was as much a curiosity to them as they were to me—an American woman traveling alone in Scotland. So, Stuart—that was the patron sitting alone—asked if he could sit beside me, and our conversation continued. Afterwards, he and I walked to another pub down the street for a beer before I went on to the Tattoo—alone, mind you. What's important is that, by being open to the experience and waiting for a place in which I felt comfortable, an ordinary meal turned into a very pleasant beginning to my vacation.

Away from home

When you're away from home is the easiest time to have a meal out alone. After all, you're in a different location, surrounded by strangers and run very little risk of seeing anyone you know. Just like with the movie experience, you can carry on a little self-talk prior to going out and remind yourself that, one, *What makes you think anyone is looking at you?* and, two, *What do you care if they are? It's no one's business but yours anyway!*

Now, where to go? It seems obvious to me that *what* you're hungry for should dictate what kind of restaurant you'll go to. And, by the way, you should be going to a *real* restaurant, not one of those fast-food places with a drive-thru lane, giveaway toys and indoor playgrounds. You're a grown-up, remember, and should be treating yourself to a grown-up meal. Once you know what you want to eat, you have several options to finding a place. "Let your fingers do the walking" and use that big yellow book that your hotel provides. Ask the concierge or a hotel employee for recommendations. The locals are another great source you can turn to for advice on where to dine. Or just drive around to see what catches your fancy. The next thing to consider if you're uncomfortable about going into a restaurant alone is *when* to go. Stay away during the peak hours, going a little before or after these busy times so there will be less of an "audience." However, I suggest you consider going during the peak hours anyway. The truth is, you're more likely to blend in with the crowd when it's busy and not be as obvious as you would be in a half-empty restaurant. Besides, part of the enjoyment of this experience is the people-watching, so the busier it is, the more people for you to watch!

When you arrive, chances are you'll be greeted by a host who will ask "How many in your party?" or some variation. *It's very important how you answer here.* Do NOT say, "Just one." Can't you hear how pathetic that sounds? It's almost apologetic! No, no, no! You are not "just" you—you are YOU! Look the host straight in the eyes and say, "One please" as if it's the most common thing in the world to you. This is a bit of a pet peeve with me. I find myself correcting a host who initially asks, "Just one?", with the response, "No, one please." It usually goes right over his or her head, but *I* feel better.

When you are shown to your table or booth, take the seat in which you'll feel most comfortable on this first excursion alone. If that means sitting with your back to the room, by all means feel free to do so. My guess is that as time progresses, you'll be facing the crowd and enjoying the scenery. And if you feel inclined to do so right from the start, good for you. Personally, I need to face as much of a room as possible. I don't like having people coming up behind me or not being able to see what's going on around me. Kind of like a gangster who won't sit with his back to a room in fear of being attacked from behind by his enemy. (Boy, an analyst could probably have a field day with that one!)

Occupying your time between bites

Okay, the extra place settings have been removed, you've been served your water or drink and your order has been placed. Now what do you do? Twiddling your thumbs is always an option, but take it from someone who knows, it doesn't keep your interest for long! Some people have asked if taking a book to read at the table is acceptable. Personally, I don't find anything wrong with that—a good book and a good meal are great companions. You may even find this a way to ease yourself into the dining alone experience. Just don't get in the habit of using the book to "hide" behind. Eventually, go out and leave the book at home.

Let's assume you don't have a book to occupy your time between bites. What else can you do? I had an incredible eating experience that I'd like to share with you that I think is worth repeating whenever time and circumstances permit. I was attending a week-long seminar at the Option Institute in the Berkshire Mountains of Massachusetts in the spring of '91. The seminar, called *Inward Bound*, was very introspective and personal. On the fourth day, we were instructed to eat a light lunch because we would be served a special snack during the afternoon session. When we reconvened in the cabin meeting room after our afternoon break, we were further instructed to observe complete silence, find our seats and not to begin eating until told to do so.

In our absence during the break, our floor seats had been rearranged in two long rows, facing each other, with a runner down the middle like a tablecloth. On this had been beautifully arranged at each place a simple, black plate of fruit, crackers and cheese, as well as a glass of water and a linen napkin. For the next ninety minutes or so, the only voice heard was that of our instructor, Barry "Bears" Kauffman, co-founder of the Institute, as he took us through an eating phenomenon that can only be described as "sensual."

With soft, instrumental music playing in the background, Barry guided us through the snack using all of our senses. First, we looked at the plate of food, noting how the colors complemented each other and how artfully the food had been arranged. As we picked up each slice, we felt its texture with our fingertips—the fuzzy skin of the kiwi, the slimy banana, the smooth grape. We then held the morsel up to our nostrils and inhaled its aroma, noticing what kind of responses our bodies had to the different types of food. Placing the morsel on our tongues, we didn't bite it but allowed it to slowly dissolve as we moved it from one part of our mouths to another. We experienced varying tastes and textures–sweet and sour, bitter and bland, warm and cold, mushy and crisp, smooth and grainy—until the transformed morsel slithered down our esophagi to settle gently in our stomachs.

The experience was very pleasurable and gave me an appreciation for how satisfying just a small portion of food can be if eaten slowly and attentively. Too often, we "inhale" our meals because of our busy schedules or don't even notice what or how much we've eaten because we're distracted by the television show we're watching, the magazine we're reading or the conversation around the table. We may not even stop and sit down to eat, but stand at the kitchen sink or eat one-handed while driving. And I'm guilty of all of the above! But, eating out alone in a restaurant is a good place to practice this kind of deliberate dining. No one need know you're doing it—as long as you don't use your fingers to pick up the mashed potatoes!

Anyway, back to your table. I mentioned earlier that part of this experience is "people watching." Be sure to glance around you during your meal and notice the other patrons. Maybe you can create imaginary stories about them. The man and woman sitting at the next table who have said hardly one word to each other since they sat down—did they have an argument before arriving or have they been together for so long that they're comfortable in their shared silence? There's the family in the corner booth with the noisy, restless youngsters—are the parents really oblivious to the disturbance their children are causing or have they learned to block out their cries? Or what about that gentleman sitting alone near the window? A traveling businessman—or a spy? Let your imagination soar!

And what are they thinking about you, this attractive woman or man eating alone in a crowded restaurant? *Must be a very confident person who enjoys the pleasure of her or his own company. Wish*

I could be that confident! See, your singular dining experience is a success!

Having leisurely consumed your meal, don't feel compelled to rush off. Sit back and relax, allowing the magnitude of what you've accomplished to sink in, basking in your success. Order another drink and have a private toast to yourself for a job well done! You can pay the bill and walk out with your head up, knowing that you've mastered yet another activity with yourself.

In the neighborhood

I'll admit that going out to dinner alone where I lived was not something I thought about doing often. After a day at the office, I'd look forward to going home, kicking off my shoes and doing whatever was on my agenda for that evening, which usually included cooking a meal for myself. Other times, dinner out was a date or a social event when I could meet with a friend or two to catch up on our lives and enjoy each other's company. Still again, special occasions might have meant going out for a meal with family members. Rarely did I think about going out by myself to eat—it was usually an afterthought like, *I should go out more often and treat myself to a lunch or dinner alone.* But I'd tend to forget these good intentions.

Yet, there are times when I have a hunger for a particular restaurant's fare. Like the fettuccine Alfredo with grilled chicken breast at the Outback restaurant. Or the Philly cheese steak sandwich at Maxwell's. When this happens, I'll admit that I may first think about who I can call to go with me. As social beings, this is a natural impulse. Usually, this means setting a future date to go there together, postponing the immediate urge to satisfy those special hunger pangs. But sometimes my good intentions to "go it alone" synchronize with this immediate urge, and I find myself telling some host, "one please."

Obviously, the same guidelines apply when dining out in your own neighborhood as when doing so away from home—when to go, where to sit, what to do at the table. The only difference is that you *may* run into someone you know. Would this bother you? It would bother some people because they feel the need to explain to this person or persons *why* they're by themselves. It's such an unusual phenomena in our society that their self-consciousness is immediately aroused and maybe even their defenses. How do you think you'd handle the situation? How do you think *I'd* handle the situation?

If you're thinking that I'd be calm and unabashed when confronted with acquaintances during a "dining alone" experience, think again. I was raised in the same society as you, after all, and I am aware of assumptions that could be made about a person who's alone. Despite all my conscious efforts to overcome feelings of self-consciousness associated with being alone, on occasion I can still get those little "butterflies" that flutter around in the center of my anatomy when I realize I've been "caught." It's a natural reaction, I guess, but one that I've learned to stifle so that the moment of apprehension is just that—a fleeting moment, if that long.

Whenever I do meet someone I know in a restaurant, I smile and acknowledge them and maybe share a few pleasantries. If asked point blank what I'm doing there all by myself, I simply answer nicely, and honestly, that I wanted a particular dish or felt like being out in public or needed to get out of the house or just wanted to spend some time alone. No further explanation is needed. No excuses. No long, drawn out justification. After all, I don't really *owe* anyone an explanation for my actions, do I? This may sound callous, but it's true. And if you can remember that, you can keep your responses to such inquiries to a friendly minimum. And, by the way, if this is your first experience dining alone and they ask you to join them, graciously decline. You've gotten this far and shouldn't abandon the experience just for the sake of what others may think.

Zanne Schmalzer wrote an article entitled, "Dining Solo? Join the Crowd," for the MSN City Guides in June 2007. You'll find it in Appendix A. I particularly liked that she recognizes the bartender as a "built-in companion" for the solo diner.

All in all, the dining out alone experience can be a very enjoyable one. I hope you'll try it for yourself—and I mean that literally, *for your self*. Bon appetit!

Chapter Four - Recommendations

1. Hold another "self talk" conversation about why you should or shouldn't dine out alone. What reasons crop up? What excuses? What anxieties? How do they manifest themselves in you—butterflies in your stomach? Sweaty palms? Giddiness? Excitement? Dread?

2. Notice the similarities and differences in your response to the above questions as compared to your responses for going alone to the movies. You may see a pattern emerging, such as, being overly concerned about what others are thinking about you or feeling thrilled at the prospect even though you haven't yet gotten up the courage to do it.

3. If you've already dined out alone, was your previous experience away from home or in your own neighborhood? You might want to try the other as a new experience.

   Think about your first time. How did you feel? What was your self-talk about? Have you gone again since? If not, ask yourself *why* not and do Step 1 above. However, if this has become a regular event for you, try this the next time you go. See if there's anyone else in the restaurant that's all alone. Observe how the person behaves and try to decide if this is a "first timer." Maybe a smile or a word of encouragement from you will ease this person's dis-ease. If nothing else, you'll feel good knowing how far you've come that a meal out alone is no longer a traumatic event. And remembering what you learned from your first experience will help you tackle some of the other experiences later in this book.

4. Make a dinner (or breakfast or lunch) date with yourself! Decide on a day and time when you'll feel comfortable going. Decide on the restaurant and find out if they require reservations for dinner. Write the date on your calendar. If it helps, think about what you'll wear. Anything that will help you prepare for this date with yourself!

5. Go out to eat! Don't forget to tell the host that you want a "table for one, please." Have an "in body" experience, being aware of what's going on outside and, more importantly, *inside* of you. What are your feelings? What are your thoughts? How do you feel physically?

6. Remember to give yourself a pat on the back when you leave the restaurant!

7. Was it good for you? If so, great! Now, keep it up. If it wasn't so good for you, remember, that's great, too! Give yourself credit for doing something that took a lot of courage. Think about why it wasn't a good experience for you and make some changes in your planning. A different day or time. A different restaurant or seat. A different kind of restaurant that draws a different type of crowd. Whatever will work for you is appropriate. It's *your* experience!

Suggestions

1. If you get reruns of the television show, *Frasier*, keep an eye out for the episode when he goes out to dine alone. It's sure to make any experience you have seem dull in comparison.

2. I couldn't think of any books or movies that depict the plight
    of this experience. But, in keeping with the title of this chap-
    ter, I do have a movie to recommend. It's a quiet little movie
    starring Jon Voight and Richard Crenna called "Table for
    Five." It takes place on a cruise ship where a divorced, dead-
    beat dad takes his three children on a vacation in the hopes
    of getting to know them better. He has an extra place set at
    their table—hence, table for five—for someone they might
    meet who's alone and would like to join them. Of course, he
    has his own agenda as to who that person should be, while the
    children keep finding stray septuagenarians to join them.

CHAPTER FIVE

A CLASS ACT

I f I could find a way to make a living being a student, I'd do it
in a heartbeat. What can I say—I love going to school! I have
taken classes of one kind or another most of my adult life. The
interesting thing is that I dropped out of college in '67 after just six
weeks—bored and homesick. I'd gone to Pasadena (California) City
College and was living with an aunt and uncle. I hadn't planned on
going to college until my aunt called to suggest I live with them and
attend the local two-year school. Now, what seventeen-year-old girl
from Ohio in her right mind would turn down an offer to live in
Southern California? It was the Sixties, when surfer shows, beach
blanket movies and Beach Boy songs inundated our lives. How could
I say no? But after a summer in the sun, I realized that I really didn't
want to be in college after all, so I headed back home.

In truth, I've never regretted my decision. Instead, I've discovered in myself a hunger for knowledge that has resulted in me taking
classes on a "want to know" basis. I enrolled in Pace University in New
York in the early '80s. While there, I took a number of psychology
classes, a criminal law class and, my favorite, drawing. From 1992 to
1997, I was a full-time, then part-time, student at Youngstown State

University in Ohio. I've changed my major four times and have minor degrees in psychology, early childhood education and English. But I have yet to get a degree. You see, for me it's not about having that diploma. It's about learning, about interacting with the professors and students. It's about improving my life by improving my mind.

But what does all this have to do with being alone, you may ask. Well, it isn't easy finding someone to take a class with you when you're the only one interested in the subject matter. Or to find someone who wants to commit the time to attending classes regularly for six, eight or ten weeks at a time. So, you find yourself making a choice: not taking the class because you're afraid of going alone or throwing caution to the wind and taking the class anyway.

What's the *worst* that can happen? No one's making you go, so if you really don't like the class after a while, drop out! There's no truancy system for delinquent adult students, so no need to worry about "getting caught." But on the other side of that question is what's the *best* that can happen? You might actually enjoy yourself, learn something interesting, share what you already know with others, and feel good about yourself. Sounds good to me—what about you? Are you ready to sign up yet?

Credit vs. non-credit courses

There are numerous options available to you for classes. The first is to decide if you want to take ones that may contribute toward a degree. I'm not going to talk about actually going to university with the sole purpose of getting a degree. That's a different kind of learning focus that only you can determine is right or not for you at this time. What I'm referring to are the occasional credit courses that interest you that you may or may not tack onto a degree program at some time. You can either take these courses for the credits or audit them. Auditing classes means that you pay the regular price, attend the class, but are not graded on the class–no tests or graded projects unless you choose to take them for your own gratification— which can take the pressure off and allow you to simply enjoy the experience.

The other type of class is the non-credit course, often called 'continuing education' at the university level. You can find these at universities, high schools, churches, sewing centers, museums, fitness centers, social clubs and plenty more places in your community. I am the self-proclaimed "queen" of non-credit courses, having taken countless ones over the years for various and sundry reasons. Like the time I took English-style horseback riding lessons for four weeks so I could go riding on the moors during my vacation to England. The little riding I had done over the years, including spending a week on a ranch in Colorado, which you'll hear about later, was on western saddles. My only other experience on an English saddle was when a co-worker, Sam, invited me riding with his family one Sunday in the early '70s.

When he led out the mare that I was to ride, I asked where the saddle was. I was used to plenty of leather and wool between me and the horse and a nice, big horn to hold onto. He assured me I'd get used to the smaller English saddle in no time and probably end up preferring it. Well, I wasn't so sure, but I was willing to give it a try. I mounted the mare, and we all headed down the driveway, across the country road and into a field at a nice, leisurely trot.

So far, so good. Then, Sam's horse, the mare's frisky two-year-old offspring who was in the lead, decides to speed up to a canter, then a gallop. Mama, of course, follows suit. But within minutes I realized something was terribly wrong. My body and the saddle were sliding precariously to the left. I was riding side saddle–literally! I held onto the horse's neck, yelling for her to stop between screams for help. In what seemed like forever, but was really just a matter of minutes, Sam had pulled up beside me, stopped the mare and helped me to the ground. His apologies for the loose girth were sincere enough, but he couldn't hide the laughter in his eyes. Luckily, I could eventually laugh about it, too, although I've stuck with western-style saddles since, except for that trip to England. And I made sure I knew how to ride English-style before I went.

Some of the other non-credit courses I've taken over the years include: acting; aerobics; ballet; compassionate listening; CPR; fencing; ice skating; interior design; literacy tutoring; massage therapy; metaphysics—beginning and advanced; palm reading; photography; sign language—beginning and intermediate; swimming—beginning, intermediate and advanced; tai chi; tarot card reading; transcendental meditation; wood sculpting; and, writing, including poetry, professional and creative. My most recent lessons have been in alpine skiing, improvisational comedy, blues harmonica and Italian. For instance, let's take skiing...

On September 16, 2000, I arrived in Park City, Utah, and I got a job for the winter at Deer Valley Resort. I had skied over twenty years before when I lived in New York and spent time on the mountains in Vermont. But it was more an activity to share with friends than a sport I enjoyed or mastered—something to do before the bars opened. When I got rid of my ski equipment in 1980, I figured I'd seen the last of a ski run or chair lift. So, you can imagine my surprise when—with a lot of persuasion from my co-workers–I decided to start all over again, take a lesson and see if skiing in the west really was better than skiing back east, as the locals professed. That was in December. In three short months, I advanced from a First-timer to an Intermediate skier and can attest to the fact that skiing is much more fun in the western mountains, at least for me. To my surprise, I loved it! It became a joke in the office–if I wasn't at my desk, I must be out taking a ski break!

What's important to know from this is that skiing is a great 'alone' sport. I spent many hours riding the chair lifts and skiing down the Deer Valley mountains by myself, usually on my Sunday afternoon ski breaks, but sometimes on my two days off as well. Oh, I skied with friends and instructors on their days off, too, and had lots of fun doing so. But nothing can take away from that feeling I'd get when I'd stop alone at the top of a slope early in the morning before anyone else had been on that particular run. When the only sound I'd hear was the creaking of the bare aspens swaying ever so lightly in the mountain breeze. When the only marks on the slope ahead of me were the corduroy-like tracks left by the grooming machines before dawn. When I felt as one with the mountain, with the sky, with the universe. It has to be experienced to be understood.

So, getting back to non-credit courses. As I explained, I've taken quite a few over my lifetime–I'll bet I have the equivalent of several degrees or maybe even a doctorate! Do I still practice all these skills that I learned? Of course not, at least not all of the time. It's not easy finding someone to fence with on the spur of the moment. Nor am I very adept at sign language any more since I never knew anyone with whom I could share it. But once the knowledge is acquired, it can't be "unlearned." It filters into my life in subtle ways without my even being aware of it. More than anything, my life has been enriched by the experiences of those classes and by the people I've met during those experiences.

What interests you?

Are you ready to enroll in a class? If this is your first time and the prospect really intimidates you, then pick something you're already knowledgeable in. Do you sew? Maybe a class in a specialization, like appliqués or quilts, would suit you. Do you workout? Then try a different form from your usual one, like boxing or Tai Chi. Are you computer literate? Maybe learning a new software or focus, such as newsletter production or graphic design, would work. Whatever your current hobbies or interests, there are always more ways to expand your level of knowledge and learn new things about them.

If you're an adventurous, curious person, then something entirely different and unrelated to anything you already do is for you. For instance, fencing. What possible, practical reason could I have for taking fencing? I didn't plan on competing. I didn't know anyone who fenced. Yet, I was always drawn to those swashbuckling movies— Errol Flynn as Robin Hood or Mark Hamill as Luke Skywalker–and decided, *why not?* What I learned besides the techniques of fencing–and that I had muscles I never knew about (ouch!)–was how to concentrate in a way I hadn't done before. Not one for competitive sports, I found myself competing on a level that required full concentration on another person's actions in order to protect myself. That concentration carries through to my current alertness and ability to sense things better physically.

Go to the head of the class

Okay, you've enrolled and are going to your first class. My advice is not to sit in the back of the room, nearest the door as if preparing for a quick getaway. Try a seat near the front of the class in one of the end rows or tables. This way you can turn your body in such a way to see the whole class and feel in control of your environment. The closer you are to the instructor, the less distractions from other students and the easier to hear what's going on.

It's been my experience as an adult student that I may have incidences in my life that relate to what's being discussed in a class. Sharing this information as it applies to the lesson is a great way to participate—you become teacher as well as student. Just be sure not to abuse this privilege by "hogging" the floor with your frequent interjections. The other side of that is listening to the offerings of other students because not all of the material you will learn in an adult class is imparted by the instructor. You may even connect with another student because of similar experiences and develop a new friendship along the way.

Something to remember when taking classes is that, whether for credit or for pleasure, you have made a non-verbal commitment to the instructor and the other students that you will participate and contribute to the class. This means being on time, attending all of the classes (barring unforeseen situations), not disrupting the class by chatting with another student, turning off your cell phone (no calls or text messages!) and meeting deadlines for projects or assignments. The dynamics of the class are as much a part of the learning experience as the material being taught. If you decide that you truly do not want to attend the class after one or two sessions, let the instructor know and stop going. Sporadic or indifferent attendance can detract from the class for the rest of the students.

Enriching your life through continued education has a potent effect on your experience of being alone, of being with yourself. If you truly want to enjoy the pleasure of your own company, then doing all you can to make that "company" more interesting is to your own advantage.

Chapter Five - Recommendations

1. It's time for more "self talk." You know what to do. Do any new feelings come up related to taking classes alone that haven't come up before? Why do you think that is? Are there latent feelings from your school days as a child or teenager that are surfacing here, feelings that are prohibiting you from enrolling in a class? If you can talk yourself through and beyond them, you'll be ready for a totally different experience as an adult student.

2. Check your community for classes that are being offered. Call local colleges, vocational schools, YW or YMCAs and have their catalogs mailed to you. Stop by fitness centers, or other centers of interest, and just observe what's going on. Get a feel for the place first, then ask about their classes.

3. Decide on a class to take and enroll. Mark your calendar. Buy a notebook, pen or other materials that may be needed for the first class.

4. The first day of school—give yourself plenty of time to get there, find a parking place, find the classroom and get a good seat. Get excited—it's going to be fun!

5. As the days or weeks of your class progress, take time to evaluate the experience. Is it better or worse than you expected? Why? What would make it a better experience for you—different subject? Different place? Different instructor? Better time or day? Keep these in mind for your next class.

6. The last day of school—congratulations! You made it! Now, don't you feel good about yourself? And even if this first experience wasn't all you'd hoped, there are plenty of other opportunities out there for you to try. Believe me, it's worth the effort in the long run!

CHAPTER SIX

WHISTLE WHILE YOU WORK...OUT!

E xercise—that eight letter "4-letter word" that most of us shy away from. We *know* it's good for us. We *know* we can't be truly healthy and fit without it. We *know*...but still we find ways to procrastinate about doing it, avoiding it like the plague. Why is that? Laziness? Fear of pain? Worry about looking silly? Physical limitations? Boredom? Don't know where to start? Whatever the reason, exercise is something we all should be doing regularly.

However, this book and this chapter are not meant to be an exposition on the benefits of exercise. I want to talk to you about the benefits of exercising *on your own*. Of course, working out with a friend or two could be the incentive that gets you moving—and, by all means, keep it up. But just like with the movies or going out to eat or other activities, a friend is not always around to accompany you. And because exercise *is* an important health-related activity, you should not talk yourself out of doing it just because you have to do it alone.

Personally, I like to workout, at least most of the time. Even when I have to talk myself into going to the gym "for just 20 minutes."

This is especially true on cold, winter evenings when I leave work at 5 o'clock in the dark. I just want to go home and hunker down in my recliner with the gas fireplace taking the chill off. I often find myself in a self-talk conversation to convince myself that, despite having to change out of all my cozy outer winter gear into skimpy gym shorts and t-shirt and then to leave the gym in my sweaty workout clothes, I will feel better in the long run. Usually, once I get there and get started, I stay longer and feel better afterwards for having done so.

I'm not going to bore you with all my exercise stories, but I will tell you when I actually started giving exercise a place in my life. It was 1978 and I was living in Suffern, New York, a little town on the west side of the Hudson River about an hour from New York City. All of my women's magazines were touting the benefits of jogging and power-walking as a way to keep—or get back—our girlish figures. The main audience for these publications was the Baby Boomer generation, who were in their mid 20s to early 30s. So I bought into the hype, bought myself a cute workout outfit and comfortable shoes and hit the streets of Suffern. I soon discovered that jogging wasn't my thing, but power-walking was, and I've been hooked ever since.

A couple years later, I was working for Xerox Corporation in Greenwich, Connecticut, and took my first step aerobic class at a local gym. Gyms were going through a change around this time, shifting from the macho, muscle-bound guys' lair to co-ed facilities where we gals could get our workouts in, too. But more about gyms later.

In 1982, Jane Fonda came out with her first workout video. Joke all you want about the "Flashdance" attire—leotards, leg warmers and sweat headbands—those workouts really worked for me and I still remember some of the moves to this day! As of this writing, Jane is 74 and has come out with her "Prime Time" workout videos, which just goes to show that we're never too old to exercise. In fact, according to Chris Crowley and Dr. Henry Lodge in their book "Younger Next Year for Women," moving is one of the most important things we can do to keep ourselves healthy as we age. They say that while we can't avoid the inevitable—aging—we can make sure that we age well and gracefully, putting off aches and pains and disease. Exercise is the vital element to maintaining a youthful lifestyle. We don't have to move the same as when we were in our 20s or 30s, but *we have to move.* Jane gets it, I get it and so should you.

Okay, I got on my soap box there for a minute but that's because I really believe in this stuff. I think a lot of this clicked for me when I took a Physiology of Exercise course at Youngstown State University in the early 90s. Between video lectures and actual sessions with a trainer, that course not only taught me how to properly lift weights, stretch, walk and use gym equipment, it taught me the 'why' behind it all. I'm a 'big picture' person, so the why really sunk in and remains a basis for how I work out today.

As I mentioned earlier, I became an avid power-walker over the years. While walking outside one day, I created a cadence for myself, imagining an army drill sergeant calling out the lines to me, as follows:

I am tall and I am thin .
> *I am tall and I am thin*

I am healthy from within.
> *I am healthy from within*

Feel those muscles churning, churn.
> *Feel those muscles churning, churn*

Feel those fat cells burning, burn.
> *Feel those fat cells burning, burn*

Pounds off
> *One, two*

Inches off
> *Three, four*

Pounds off, inches off

Gonna lose...lots more!

Okay, it's corny, but it's a motivating mantra, trust me! Feel free to use it or create your own that will keep you moving at an even pace. I even translated it into Italian when I was studying that language, but it loses something in the translation so I'll spare you that version. The point is, you've got to make whatever you do fun or it becomes tedious, and tedium can spell disaster for any workout program.

13.1 Miles

On June 3, 2006, I put my power-walking abilities to the test by signing up for my first half marathon in Salt Lake City. I had decided a couple months earlier that I wanted to challenge myself physically, and this seemed like the perfect way to do that. So I started a workout regimen to get myself ready, which included longer and longer outdoor walks to build up my endurance and increased strength training to make sure my whole body could endure this challenge.

The event began at the University of Utah, and I was feeling excited and nervous as we lined up at the starting line around 7 a.m. When the buzzer went off, so did I, with the Moody Blues' "I'm Just a Singer in a Rock and Roll Band" coming through my MP3 player to motivate me. Our route wound through the university, into residential neighborhoods, along business routes and eventually to the Gateway Center in downtown Salt Lake City. People talk about hitting a brick wall when doing long-distance activities, and I hit mine around the 10 mile post, near Liberty Park. But I pushed through it and, as I approached the 12 mile post, choked up as I realized I was actually doing this! I 'talked' to my mom and dad in my thoughts and felt them cheering me on from heaven's spectator stands. The crowds along the sidelines increased as I approached the finish line. And crossing that line was one of the best feelings I've ever felt in my life. I'd done it! I'd walked 13.1 miles–and believe me, that .1 mile makes the difference!—and completed my first half-marathon in 3 hours 34 minutes and 16 seconds! For a 56-year old woman who was never athletically inclined, this was a major achievement. And, as much as it's a physical challenge, it was probably just as much a psychological and emotional challenge. To celebrate, I'd booked a 3-1/2 hour spa experience for myself the next day and languished in every minute of it!

Since then, I've done three more half-marathons in Park City, improving my time with each event. Half, or full, marathons are ideal alone workout experiences because, even if you sign up for one with friends, you will end up alone as you all move at your own pace and get into your own zones. Then, at the end, you can all celebrate together...the best of both worlds!

Pink boxing gloves

My latest physical challenge has been to take up boxing. Not kick-boxing–tried that once and tore the medial meniscus in my right knee, which required lathroscopic surgery. I mean the "Million Dollar Baby," put-up-your-dukes boxing. I started with a trainer at my gym, just learning the moves and using gel-padded gloves to hit his hand mitts or the stand-up punching bag. Eventually, he said I was hitting hard enough that I should invest in regular boxing gloves.

I found a gym in a nearby town that was run by a female professional boxer and spent the summer of 2011 working out at her gym once a week. And I ordered by pink wraps and gloves from her. Yes, pink! Makes a statement, don't you think? Then, in the winter of 2012, I connected with a boxing trainer at my gym in Park City. Shane had boxed on the Tongan team in the 1996 Olympics. He and I meet for an hour once a week, and I really, really love it! We do core exercises for balance and for my abs—he actually drops a six-pound medicine ball on my abs from a standing position!—but most of the hour is spent doing two-minute punching rounds. I felt so clumsy and weak when I first started, but my strength and stamina have improved a lot. While I don't care if I ever compete, I enjoy how the sport works my entire body and mind. There's something liberating about hitting something as hard as you can...especially in those cute pink gloves!

What's stopping you?

So, that's my story in a nutshell. What's yours? Do you have an exercise program in place for yourself, making sure you get in at least a few days a week raising your heartbeat, burning fat and strengthening your muscles? You've probably already figured out that the important thing about this topic is that it's not so much about doing it alone as it is about *doing it*—alone or otherwise. As Nike would say, *Just do it!* (Another great motivating mantra, by the way.)

For the purpose of this book, however, I want to encourage those of you who avoid working out, going to a gym, joining a dance class or whatever because you are self-conscious about your body to do your best to overcome that self-consciousness. Believe me, I understand the feelings. Self talk is really important here because you've got to convince yourself that *you* are who matters, not everyone else. When

I see someone in the gym who is obviously new to the experience, I give her a silent "Atta-girl!" because she's *there*. She's overcome whatever fears she had, decided in favor of her health and well being and taken that all-important first step.

First and foremost for novices, *get your doctor's seal of approval before you begin any workout program*. This is a must. Find out if there are any limitations based on your physical condition and share those limitations with any trainers or instructors you work with in the future.

So, back to gyms—yes, they can be intimidating. So many firm, supple bodies. So many torturous pieces of equipment. So many reasons to turn around, head for Cold Stone Creamery and drown your trepidations in a triple-scoop chocolate sundae with the works. Yet, gyms needn't be as intimidating as all that. Take your time to check out the ones in your town to find the perfect fit for you. Have someone take you on a tour of the facility and explain the membership, classes and other amenities. Ask if you can try out the place with a free first visit before committing to a membership, and some are free.

Once you've settled on the *where*, get yourself a *who* – a personal trainer, that is. You don't have to use this person every time you workout, but if you're new to the gym environment you *must* be taught how to use the equipment properly to avoid injury—the financial investment is well worth it. Personal trainers are great for creating a workout plan that matches your goals and abilities. They will give you that little push you need to step outside your comfort level and work a little harder or try something new, while making sure you don't overdo it.

Most gyms offer classes that you can participate in for free or a minimal cost if you are a member. Zumba, spinning, aerobics, yoga, kickboxing, swimming and more are available to mix up your routine. Going to these alone, you become lost in the crowd because no one is really paying attention. You're all there for the same reason, will share in the energy, and then go your separate ways when it's done. But that shared energy will stay with you for hours afterwards, both physically and psychologically.

Moseying

I'm about to take a complete 180-degree turn here and talk to you about moseying. Where power-walking, running and other forms of exercise are great workouts for your body, moseying is a great workout for your mind and spirit. And it's just as important to exercise those parts of your being as well.

My first job after high school was working for a bank in my hometown of Warren, Ohio. After several years in the loan department, I transferred to the newly-formed computer department as a programmer in 1970. Computers were the latest technology, and I got in on the ground floor when the bank decided to create their own department instead of timesharing with an out-of-town bank. Anyway, another employee brought into the department was a mild-mannered family man named Sam B. Sam taught me to mosey.

Second National Bank was across from the southwest corner of the town square. The mammoth courthouse, constructed in 1895 in the Richardson Romanesque design, was on the north side of the square; and a park, complete with gazebo and pathways, stretches out from its front doors. During our lunch hours, Sam and I would sometimes walk around town and through the park. Invariably, he would grab my arm and make me slow down, telling me to mosey and enjoy the walk. I tend to have a long, fast stride, which I think I got trying to keep up with my long-legged dad as a child. So I'd make a conscious effort to mosey and take in the sights and sounds around me as Sam suggested. Those lessons in moseying stuck with me, and I found myself teaching others the art of moseying over the years. In fact, I wrote an essay called "The Art of Moseying" that won me second place in the Midwest Writers' Conference in Canton, Ohio, in 1996. You can read it for yourself in Appendix B.

Moseying is a great alone experience because you have to concentrate in order to do it properly. Think of it as a kind of walking meditation. Learn to enjoy your surroundings and heighten your senses. It's another form of solitude that you can later share with a friend once you've mastered its nuances.

Chapter Six - Recommendations

1. For those of you who already have a workout routine, whether alone or with friends, by all means continue with it. Remember, this chapter isn't about exercise as much as it's about not avoiding exercise just because you'd have to do it alone. Just for fun, you might want to challenge yourself to doing something different by yourself for a change.

2. For those of you who *do* shy away from working out alone, this is the time for more self talk to convince yourself that it's all right and for your best interest. Use the time to get in your own zone and notice what your body is going through—your breathing, your flexibility, your speed, your endurance. What movements challenge you more than others?

3. Up the ante and register for a local event, such as, a 5K (3.1 miles), 10K (6.2 miles), half marathon (13.1 miles) or full marathon (26.2 miles). Start with the short events and work your way up to the others...or be satisfied with completing just one if that's what works for you! Again, my intention for recommending this is not so much for the obvious physical benefits, but as an ultimate alone experience, something you can do *for* yourself *by* yourself. The psychological and spiritual benefits of completing that first event will do wonders for your spirit.

4. For women, upper body strength is usually in need of improvement. Afraid of becoming too muscular? Learn how to use free weights properly to tone up, not bulk up. Check out other equipment, such as, resistance bands or kettle balls. Variety in

what you use and what you do will make your workouts more interesting and fun.

5. Mosey around the neighborhood! Don't forget to allow yourself time to exercise your mind and spirit so that your entire being will be synchronized to energy, awareness and wellness.

Suggestions

1. "Younger Next Year for Women" and "Younger Next Year" by Chris Crowley and Henry S. Lodge, M.D.

CHAPTER SEVEN

THE OVERNIGHTER OR THE WEEKEND GETAWAY

Sometimes, after a long, grueling week at work or a particularly hectic week with the family and children, do you just need a little time to yourself? Do you need some space in which to unwind and lose track of time with no deadlines, pressures or interruptions? Taking an overnight or weekend trip alone is a good way to spend time with yourself.

My first weekend trip alone was over Thanksgiving weekend in 1981. If you traditionalists out there are wondering why I wasn't spending this major American holiday with my family, let me explain. My family lived in Warren, Ohio—where I was born and raised—but I was living in Bedford Hills, New York. Since I always flew home in December for Christmas, I didn't feel the need to make the trip there one month earlier. Nor did I feel like making that eight-hour drive across Pennsylvania when the weather and roads could turn on you at that time of the year. You do *not* want to be driving through those Pennsylvania mountains in a snowstorm! I had my share of invitations from friends in the New York area to spend the holiday with them and their families, which I usually did. But this year, I decided to go it alone.

I headed east to Mystic, Connecticut, a small, quaint harbor town just before the Rhode Island border. (For you film aficionados, it's the same Mystic featured in the movie, *Mystic Pizza*.) I left Bedford Hills around eleven o'clock on Thanksgiving Day and enjoyed the two-hour drive on Interstate 95, where traffic was at a minimal. Guess all the folks were already at their final destination, watching Macy's Thanksgiving parade.

When I got off the exit, there wasn't much in the way of driver amenities. If I recall, there was one family-style restaurant and a full-service gas station, with modest signs pointing south toward the town of Mystic, Mystic Seaport and the Mystic Aquarium. Today, when you get off that same exit, you are deluged with fast food restaurants, self-service gas stations and a mini-mall consisting of those cutesy shops that give tourists the impression they are "one of a kind," when in fact they can be found at interstate exits across the country in one form or another. I'm glad I went in '81!

On the drive to town, I passed the aquarium and Mystic Seaport, a reconstruction of what the original town was like during the 1700's. Many of the houses I passed had plaques on them, identifying their original owners over two hundred years earlier. The road took me right to my destination–the Whaler's Inn in downtown Mystic, right next to the drawbridge. Yes, a real, honest-to-goodness drawbridge! I had to register at a little desk in a storefront lobby, then walk outside to the door leading to the second floor rooms. The stairway was narrow, with uneven steps and threadbare carpeting. With a little imagination, I could see sailors of yore clomping up those steep, narrow stairs after months at sea, their duffel bags slung over their shoulders, looking forward to a hot meal, a tankard of ale and a good night's sleep in a real bed.

After unpacking and freshening up, I ventured out to find a restaurant for dinner. I walked across the drawbridge and found a pleasant restaurant about a block from the inn. The place was busy–it was nice to see that I wasn't the only person eating out on Thanksgiving! I couldn't help but wonder, as I sat at my table and looked around at the other guests, what their "stories" were. Why were they eating at this particular restaurant in Mystic, Connecticut, on Thanksgiving day in 1981? Were they traveling through the area or did they come to Mystic intentionally like I did? Were they locals who preferred dining out to preparing the traditional turkey dinner at home? There were several loners, like me, and I remember thinking we should all sit together and make our own little "family" table! This is part of what traveling alone is about—people watching and creating scenarios for the people you watch.

Close to home

When planning your first short excursion, you don't have to venture far from home. An inn or resort in your own town can be just as private as one two hours away. Personally, I prefer to put distance between me and my usual "stomping grounds"—it's a psychological advantage.

In October of '88, I decided to spend my birthday weekend at Punderson State Park, a resort about forty-five minutes north of Warren, Ohio. My divorce was finalized in September, and I needed the time away to regroup. Punderson is one of those nearby places that we sometimes overlook because it is so close to home. And it was just right for me that October.

My room in the main lodge overlooked the back lawns that sloped down to the lake. There was a gorgeous central fireplace in the lounge area off the main lobby, where I curled up with a book and wrote some letters to distant friends. I spent the days hiking the park trails under the vibrant canopy of trees awash in their richest autumn colors. All in all, it was a perfect refuge.

My idyllic weekend was not without its share of adventure, however. Early Saturday evening I drove to the far side of the lake to take photographs of the sunset over the lake and lodge. I parked in an empty lot near the RV campgrounds and headed for the lake shore.

The sunset was breathtaking! I got a lot of really good shots, including some that my brother calls "artsy-fartsy." The last rays of the sun dipped behind the lodge as I headed back to my car. As I reached inside my jeans pocket for my keys, I got an awful feeling in the pit of my stomach when suddenly I realized my keys were inside my camera bag—which was on the front seat of my locked car! At the last minute, I had decided to leave the bag, but forgot to retrieve the keys before locking up. Now what?

I allowed myself a few minutes of self-recrimination and cursing before deciding the best course of action. This was a *disadvantage* to traveling alone in the off-season when no one is there with you to share those unforeseen problems! Anyway, I decided to walk through the almost-deserted campgrounds and solicit the aid of some campers. I felt like Goldilocks—no one home in camper number one or in camper number two, but camper number three was "just right." A retired couple from Michigan was sitting in lawn chairs, enjoying the quiet evening, when Little Miss Not-So-Bright approaches with her tale of woe and plea for a wire hanger. Instead of the hanger, Mr. Michigan called the park rangers' station—was this one smart "bear" or what? They also walked me back to my car to wait for the ranger to arrive. Good Samaritans *do* exist!

The good news was that less than five minutes later, a patrol car pulled up with two park rangers. The bad news was they'd been just down the road when the call came in from dispatch and they didn't have that bar gadget with them to unlock the car door. Rather than leave me waiting alone in the dark, I went back with them in the car.

Now for the *really* bad news—I had to sit in the back seat! Never having been in a police car before, I was unprepared for the claustrophobic feeling that immediately came over me. There was a steel grid between me and the front seat, my knees were crushed into the passenger seat in front of me and there were no inside handles on the doors! I was trapped, and I had to concentrate hard on my breathing in order to keep myself from screaming out. Talk about a deterrent for crime!

Anyway, when we arrived at the ranger station, the second ranger stayed behind, so I moved to the front seat and was able to breath regularly again. When we arrived back at my car, my "lone ranger" had the car door unlocked in a matter of seconds and, with a hardy "Hi-Ho-Silver" was soon headed back to the ranger station. Okay, maybe that last part was in my imagination, but I couldn't help thinking of that parting shot on the television series as the silver patrol car pulled away. Within minutes, I was on my way back to the main lodge, with yet another story to add to my "Travels with Susan" repertoire.

Touchstones

After that first visit to Mystic, I made a point of returning there now and then. As a frequent visitor to a place, you become a "regular," someone who is recognized by the locals of restaurants and shops that you visit. It creates a friendly tone to the trip—you're traveling alone, yet you have some "touchstones" who make you feel comfortable and welcome. Traveling alone doesn't mean having to feel like a stranger everywhere you go. Making new friends, even those you only see occasionally, is part of the experience.

Another place that I frequented during the early '80s was Newport, Rhode Island, about an hour east of Mystic. You have to drive over this long, high expansion bridge to get to Newport, which is on an island. This is the same Newport where Jackie Bouvier spent her childhood on her family's estate, Hammersmith, and where she later married John F. Kennedy. It's the same Newport where turn-of-the-century millionaires like Vanderbilt and Astor built summer "cottages." These mansions are now open to the public for tours to help alleviate the cost of their upkeep.

While I was interested in these opulent historical sites, what really drew me to Newport was its proximity to water. I love being near water and boat docks. I love listening to the water lapping against the wooden pier pillars, to boat bells clanging as the vessels bob in the water, to sea gulls squawking as they search for scraps of fish bait. I even like the smells of the waterfront—salty air, sea life and wet wood. Visiting a place like Newport allows me to live out fantasies as well, of pirates and smugglers and swashbucklers. I think maybe I've been one of those in a past life!

My touchstone in Newport was a bartender named Pete. He worked at a place called Yesterdays—a restaurant/bar and grill during the lunch and dinner hours and a locals' music hangout in the evenings. Pete and I first met when I visited Newport for the first time with an acquaintance. I remembered him being friendly and helpful when we asked for recommendations on places to go and things to do. So, when I returned by myself the first time, I made a point of going to Yesterdays for dinner and reacquainting myself with Pete. He was about ten years younger than me, a real looker, but he and

I were "just friends." And he watched out for me when guys would approach me while I sat there at the bar.

Like the time a sailor started "chatting me up" during my first solo visit to the island. That's a phrase I learned from my Scottish husband that means–well, I think you can figure out what it means! Anyway, this guy, though nice to talk to, was really into himself and not my type. But when he invited me to dinner the next evening, I accepted. It was a knee-jerk reaction and shows how we–women, that is–are conditioned to be nice and accept invitations from "prospective partners."

But, when he went to the "little sailor's room," I admitted to myself that I didn't want to go out with him and decided to be honest with him. So, when he returned, I graciously thanked him for the invitation, but said that I'd come to Newport by myself for the sole purpose of spending time alone and decided to pass on dinner. Well, he wasn't too pleased with my response and soon departed. A minute later, Pete brought me a fresh drink "on the house." When I asked him why, he said he liked the way I handled that "jerk," as he called him, and was glad I'd turned him down. So began our relationship!

A side note here about Pete. In June 2010, I returned to Newport for a few days while vacationing on the east coast. I was pleasantly surprised to find Yesterdays still in operation and, you guessed it, Pete attending bar! When I reminded him of when we'd first met, after a few minutes I saw the "ah-ha" bulb go on in his eyes and we had a nice visit. Turns out, he'd moved around the country, married and divorced in the thirty years since we'd last seen each other, and had only recently moved back to Newport and his family. Talk about synchronicity!

The point is, traveling alone doesn't mean you have to remain alone the entire time. The choice is up to you, and making new friends is definitely a benefit you'll want to take advantage of along the way.

Hit the road

So, where do you want to go? Is there someplace near where you live that you've always thought would be a nice place to visit, but you thought was too close to home to consider for a vacation? Maybe now is the time to make those reservations and go. Or maybe you like being behind the wheel and feeling like a gypsy in a wagon with no ties to anything, so you'll want to drive a longer distance from home. And don't rule out the bus, train or plane as a means to reaching your final destination.

This first trip can be an overnighter or you can spend a few nights away, whatever you feel comfortable doing. Do you want to be pampered at a spa? Do you like to hike, ride a bicycle, ski or horseback ride? How about a game of tennis or golf? Or maybe you just want to lie out by a pool and get some sun while you read that big, thick novel you've been putting off for so long. The activities you want to do will help in deciding where you go.

Once you know where you're going, pack appropriately. And pack lightly! I can't emphasize that enough. The hint here is, once you've packed what you think you'll need, go back and unpack half of it. That's right, half of it you probably won't wear or need at all, so why lug it all around?

This especially holds true for shoes. It's been my experience that we tend to pack too many pairs of shoes, thinking we need to match every outfit or be prepared for every contingency. (Okay, this may only apply to the female gender!) Nonsense! Pack so you'll only need one, maybe two pairs of shoes—outdoor "play" shoes and indoor "dress" shoes if appropriate. Trust me, you'll get by just fine.

As for incidentals, visit your local discount drug store and buy some of those travel-size toiletries, leaving those full bottles of shampoo *et al* at home. The idea here is to leave home behind, relax and have fun. Traveling light goes a long way in helping you feel light and carefree and unencumbered, mentally, physically and spiritually.

Room service?

Ordering from room service–this one's entirely up to you. Perhaps you don't normally travel and stay in hotels that offer room service, so ordering a meal would be part of the experience for you. Then go for it! Live it up! Personally, I like ordering breakfast from room service since there's not much difference between eggs or cereal from one restaurant to another. I like to sit in my robe after having showered and washed my hair, sip my decaf coffee, nibble on my toast, devour my pancakes or poached eggs, all the while enjoying the notion that I didn't have to raise a finger or crack one egg to make this happen! Languish in the decadence!

What you don't want to do, however, is hide behind room service as a way to avoid going out to a meal by yourself. Remember what we talked about in chapter four. This is where you get to put some of those tried and true practices to further use. Chances are, you'll find it a lot easier to go out to eat by yourself now than you did at home. After all, you're on vacation and have to eat, don't you? No one would expect otherwise.

Safety first

While it may go without saying, I think it *is* important to state here that safety is a very important consideration when traveling alone, regardless of how long you're gone or where you're going. Women especially are vulnerable because we've been brought up to be innately—and inanely—nice to people. There are too many stories on the nightly news about women who were raped or killed because they didn't follow their gut instincts when they felt afraid. Why? Because they didn't want to offend the guy or give the impression that they weren't nice. Screw that!

Fear speaks to us through our bodies when our safety is in jeopardy. That feeling in the pit of your stomach. The hairs rising up on the back of your neck. Your increased heart rate and sweaty palms. All warning signals that 'something ain't right here!' LISTEN! Pay attention to these signs and react appropriately.

The fear of doing something or going some place by yourself may trigger similar physical reactions. Learn to recognize the difference between endangerment and being out of your comfort zone. Then you can enjoy your trips to their fullest.

Balance

Are some of you still questioning the value of spending a night or weekend alone? Is there some hesitation as to whether the benefits outweigh the time, cost and effort? Perhaps Leonardo da Vinci could assist you in making your final analysis.

> *Every now and then go away,*
> *have a little relaxation,*
> *for when you come back*
> *to your work*
> *your judgment will be surer;*
> *since to remain constantly at work*
> *will cause you to lose power*
> *of judgment.*

Go some distance away
because the work appears smaller
and more of it
can be taken in at a glance
and a lack of harmony
or proportion
is more readily seen.

Leonardo da Vinci

(1452-1519)

In his book "Wisdom of the Ages," Dr. Wayne Dyer refers to this poem of da Vinci's in his chapter entitled "Balance." He says, *"It seems to me that highly productive people have a great sense of balance and harmony in their lives. They are thoroughly familiar with pacing and knowing when to retreat and clear their heads of the immediate concerns. The key word here is "balance." To avoid being consumed by anything, you must be able to walk away from it. In the process of walking away, you begin to see your work or family or project from a perspective that 'appears smaller' according to Leonardo."* (Dyer 51-54)

Detachment from your every day life, no matter how mundane or hectic, allows you to create the balance referred to here. You get to take a breather and relax. If there are problems you've been struggling with, relationships you need to explore or decisions you've been putting off, going off alone somewhere can help you get the proper perspective on the situation. If nothing else, it will help you clean out the cobwebs so you can return with a clear mind, ready to tackle whatever comes your way.

So, whenever you're ready, wherever you go, for however long you're gone, remember—this is *your* time to be with yourself. Make the most of it and enjoy!

Chapter Seven - Recommendations

1. Guess what? It's time to talk to yourself again. You should be getting really good at this process by now. What thoughts come to mind about this step that didn't show up with the other exercises? What fears? Or are you feeling more sure of yourself now, having tried some other things on your own? Perhaps you're actually looking forward to this!

2. Decide on where you would like to go for this first excursion. If possible, select a place that you can drive to within a few hours. If you don't drive, how about a bus trip? You could even have a friend or family member take you to your destination and pick you up later. The point is to keep the preparation as easy as possible—don't get bogged down in travel arrangements or reservations.

3. Don't forget my suggestions about packing—keep it light! And only use room service as a treat, not a shield.

4. Remember when you were a child, how easily you could play "make believe?" As children, we could come up with some pretty incredible play scenarios, couldn't we? Well, why not let that child in you play "make believe" again? Create a scenario about who you are, where you are, why you are there— let your imagination run wild!

   Let's say you're at bed-and-breakfast inn, sitting in a wicker lounge on the wrap-around porch, sipping iced tea while looking out over the sprawling lawns and colorful flower beds and watching a group of children being walked around a corral on a horseback ride. Only instead, imagine you're the owner of a horse ranch whose stables include Kentucky Derby winners and you're watching your latest acquisition, a magnificent two-year old quarter horse being put through its paces in the nearby corral by your trainer. You can hear the roar of the crowds now as the horse crosses the finish line to win you yet another trophy for your case. Sound crazy? So what! Only you will know that you are playing this little daydreaming game, so what's the harm? But I guarantee you, you will find yourself giggling to yourself and feeling care-free in no time.

5. Just because you're on an "alone" excursion doesn't mean you can't mingle with the other guests and enjoy their company. You don't have to be a hermit or a social misfit—remember my opening line of this book? That's not your objective. Rather, you are learning to spend time away from your safety nets while creating a broader world in which you can live. So by all means, make new friends! Chances are you will surprise them when you tell them you are alone, and maybe even inspire someone to try it sometime! You will go from student to teacher by your brave example—and feel really great about yourself as well!

6. Home again! So, how was it? What did you particularly enjoy? What did you find particularly difficult? What could you do differently next time to improve the experience— *will* there be a next time? Were you able to achieve any balance, resolve any issues or learn anything about yourself? If nothing else, did you have fun? Because, in the end, that's what matters!

Suggestions

All of these books are perfect for a short getaway—they're easy reads that provide inspiring and enjoyable tidbits on life.

1. Any of the books referenced at the end of Chapter 1.

2. "A Short Guide to a Happy Life" by Anna Quindlen

3. "Don't Sweat the Small Stuff: and It's All Small Stuff" by Richard Carlson

CHAPTER EIGHT

THE VACATION

O kay, I'll admit that during this phase, the "going it alone" process may get a little tougher. I'll also admit that there will be moments during the longer vacation when you may be asking yourself what the heck you're doing there all alone! Hey, some things are just more fun when shared with a friend! The thing is, we all have different moments when this is true. While I may love power-walking along a mountain trail all by myself, completely tuned into the environment around me and into my body as it moves through its vigorous routine, I know there are those amongst you who would miss having that walking companion next to you, matching you stride for stride as you move along the trail. On the other hand, going to a baseball game alone—even if my favorite team, the New York Yankees, is playing—doesn't appeal to me, where someone else might not give it a second thought.

So, why would you want to take a vacation alone, you may be asking. For me, the answer is the same as for when going to a movie alone— sometimes I want to go to a place that no one else is interested in. Take my first vacation alone. I wanted to go to a ranch in the west and spend the week horseback riding, but I couldn't find anyone remotely interested in accompanying me! I almost decided against the trip, but I finally convinced myself that I could do it. I could spend a whole week alone and enjoy myself.

Riding tall

I did some research at the library—this was in the pre-Internet days of 1982—and got the names of some ranches in Colorado that sounded interesting. After making some phone calls and perusing brochures, I settled on a placed called the Don K Ranch in south-central Colorado, an hour or so west of Pueblo. Nestled in the San Isabel National Forest in the Rocky Mountains, it offered spectacular views, great home-style meals and horseback rides twice a day. Sounded like what I was looking for!

I planned this trip for the second week in June, which was their "pre-season" time. There are a lot of considerations as to *when* you take your vacation in regards to whether you travel to your destination during its "on" or "off" season. Rates will vary based on the dates you visit, as will availability due to the number of guests. Also, there may be less activities scheduled during the "off" season times, such as concerts, plays and tours; and, some restaurants and shops may not yet be opened. You have to decide what's important to you, what you can live with and without, before picking the dates of your trip. I tend to travel more during the "off" seasons, for cost reasons as well as wanting to avoid crowds of tourists, driving and parking headaches and long waits at restaurants or activities.

I flew into Denver, where I visited a friend for two days first. Then I took a bus to Pueblo and was met by the owner of the ranch, Don K. himself. We connected with two other guests, a sixty-something couple from southern California, and headed west for the hour plus drive. We traveled on a paved four-lane highway, then a paved two-lane road and finally a winding dirt road through the foothills of the Rockies. As we came within miles of the ranch, Don explained that a Charles Bronson movie was filmed on the property, although I can't for the life of me remember which one.

My room was in a four-unit cabin and had knotty pine walls, faded prints of western scenes, a lamp with a base of some kind of animal antlers and a red and green plaid bedspread with ruffles. Pretty much what I would expect in this western setting, and I made myself at home for my week-long stay. That evening, we—the couple from California, Don, his wife (I think her name was Betty.), a couple of their grown children who helped around the ranch and I—had a home-style meal around a big dining room table, passing bowls of mashed potatoes, platters of corn on the cob and pitchers of iced tea as we got to know each other. All in all, it was a delightful beginning to my first vacation by myself.

That week, I got my money's worth of horseback riding and some! Monday morning, the wranglers, John and Curly (I swear, that was his name!), matched me up with a horse that I would use for the whole week. Her name was Pretty Girl, she was brown with a black mane and she had an even temperament. We got along just fine! As it turned out, the California couple and I were the only guests, so it was a small group that headed out for our first morning ride. I ended up going out for both morning and afternoon rides all week long, except for an afternoon that I spent by the pool. The California folks left after two days and no one else checked in, so it was just two wranglers and me on the morning rides.

In the afternoons, the ranch hands could join us if their chores were done. With only one guest to cook for and clean up after, you can be sure they were free and came along. We went on longer rides than usual, and I saw some sights I wouldn't have seen had I been there during their "high" season of the summer. During the afternoon rides, I found myself on some pretty adventurous trails and blazing new ones as we ventured to areas outside the normal "guest" terrain. I won't bore you with details of each ride over my seven-day stay, but suffice it to say that I had a ball! (In case you're wondering how my body took to all that riding, I was feeling the repercussions by Tuesday afternoon! Ouch, ouch and more ouch! But I soaked in a nice, hot bath that night and was ready to saddle up the next morning, albeit a little slower for a while!)

Did I wish I had someone with me? Sure, there were moments when I would have liked to chat or play cards with a friend. Moments when I felt the downside of being alone—loneliness. But those moments didn't linger, nor did I let them damper my good time. I was lucky that my first "alone" vacation experience was an active vacation, when my daily schedule consisted of breakfast, morning ride, lunch, afternoon ride and dinner, with the occasional hour here or there for reading, hiking, sketching and just plain relaxing. Also, there were lots of nice, fun people to interact with during my stay, including the occasional local visitor who came to the ranch for drinks or dinner. This helped to alleviate a lot of the pangs of loneliness.

Mount Desert Island

It was June of '95, and I had booked a cabin in the woods on Mount Desert Island off the northern coast of Maine. A co-worker had suggested the island after he and his wife had driven through the area the previous year. Again, I went to the library to do research on the island and called the chambers of commerce for Southwest Harbor and Bar Harbor, the two main towns on the island. Then, I contacted a couple of realtors, explaining that I wanted a secluded place where I could do some writing and reading while enjoying the local vistas. The place I decided on was in Hall's Quarry on the "quiet side" of the island, near Southwest Harbor. Bar Harbor is on the northeastern portion of the island and draws the most tourists during the summer season.

Something you'll have to consider when planning your vacation is whether or not you'll need a vehicle and whether you want to drive your own or rent one after your arrival. Time and finances will dictate your decision. Some locales are small enough that you can rely on local busses or trains to get around, or you can rent a bicycle or mo-ped as your means of transportation. I decided I wanted to have my own vehicle with me—a Saturn 4-door sedan at the time—so that meant I'd have a two-day drive from northeast Ohio to Maine. The advantage of this was that I could visit friends of mine in the New York/Connecticut area on my way up and back, and they provided me with free accommodations for the one-night stops.

Once again, I would be vacationing during the pre-season, so the drive up past Boston and along Route 1 was enjoyable, except for the last stretch on Route 1 in Maine. It wound through small coastal towns, and I found myself stuck behind "little old lady" drivers or trucks loaded down so they were driving ever so slowly. All this in a continuous drizzle. By the time I pulled off the road leading to my cabin, I was ready to pop open a cold brew, put up my feet and zonk out! Little did I know what awaited me as I followed the directions that took me along a dirt road through the woods to my cabin.

As I made my way, I couldn't help but wonder where in the hell I was! I was instructed to park in an open area that overlooked the cabin, the roof of which I could see through the trees and the still-falling drizzle. It was 5:00 p.m., and I was to meet the caretaker of the property, who would give me the key and help me unpack the car. My mind started wandering. I recalled that Stephen King lived in Maine and then my mind started *wondering*—was my present location an inspiration to the author for any of his macabre stories? And I couldn't help but wonder about this caretaker who was on his way.

Not a minute later, I heard, then saw, his pickup truck come through the woods. Fortunately, he turned out to be a nice guy, not at all the Jack Nicholson/*Shining* version of a caretaker I'd begun to imagine. We carried my things along the wooded trail that lead to a very nice two-bedroom cabin with a spectacular view overlooking Somes Sound. I unpacked, went grocery shopping for staples and returned to the cabin for that cold beer I'd been salivating for earlier.

But, as the sun went down behind the cabin, the view outside my picture window changed from treetops and water to my own reflection in the glass. My imagination started working again. I envisioned Michael Myers from "Halloween" standing on the deck, wearing that white mask, staring at me with that I've-got-you-now look. That wouldn't do—time to close the curtains! Only, when I went to do so, I made an awful discovery—there *were* no curtains! I felt like I was in a fish bowl, and all the creepy villains from those horror movies would soon be standing on my deck, watching me in my vulnerable state! Yikes! I immediately found some extra sheets and masking tape and proceeded to drape and create a window dressing that would never make the pages of *Better Homes and Garden*!

Yes, it was scary all alone there in that cabin that first night, especially since I had no clue what surrounded me out there in those woods or how far away the nearest neighbor was to me. Yes, I wondered if I should pack up and drive back to that Super 8 Motel I passed driving in off the mainland. Yes, I second- and third- and fourth-guessed myself about the wisdom—or lack thereof—of my decision to venture to this island alone.

But, I managed to survive the night and its strange sounds, only to wake up to see an absolutely gorgeous sunrise on the Sound. I sat on the deck with my glass of orange juice and peered through binoculars, watching a seal play in the water. Then, incredulously, I saw three fins appear—three dolphins swimming in unison as if performing a water ballet, moving effortlessly through the Sound toward the cove and the harbor. All thoughts of Michael and masks and "things that go bump in the night" faded away, never to return to scare me or make me question my decision.

Bits of wisdom

I shared these two experiences to give you some clues as to what to prepare for when planning your first vacation alone. Did you pick up on any of them? Let's review them now.

1. *Timing.* Pre- or post-season versus "in" or "high" season is a decision that will depend upon when you can take your vacation, where you're planning to go and whether finances are an issue or not for you. Rates will vary and activities will be limited/non-existent or overbooked/crowded based on the timing of your trip. Your first vacation alone may be stressful enough for you without having the added factors of people and costs. Give it a lot of thought, okay?

2. *Research Sources.* First, think about what you want to be doing on this vacation—soaking in the sun on a beach, riding the rapids down a river, lounging on a veranda with a mint julep and a good book, skiing down black diamond runs in the Rockies. Think about if you want to return to a place you've visited before or if you want to try someplace new.

Once you've decided, there are a number of sources you can draw upon to research the destination for your trip. The Internet, of course, is the "source du jour," sometimes offering more information than you can handle and making it confusing, so be discriminate. The library is another great place to gather information, and the reference librarians are always willing to be of assistance. Book stores are another source for travel guides and maps. Contact the chamber of commerce in the towns you are considering, and they will send you brochures and other literature about their locales.

3. *Transportation.* Perhaps your vacation will be driving from place to place for a week or two—great! That solves this problem. If not, you'll have to decide if you want to drive to your destination or arrive by another means of transportation and rent a car there or forego having a car at all. You'll want to factor in the cost of gas, tolls and other incidental costs related to driving. Also, think about the amount of time you want to spend "getting there" and determine if that makes a difference or not.

4. *Highways or Byways.* I mention this as a point to consider depending on what you want to get out of your drive. When I took that first trip to Maine, I took highways the entire way until I got to southern Maine. I thought I'd take scenic Route 1 up the coast for the last leg of the journey because on the map it seemed better than the more inland 95 North and I wanted to see some local color for a change.

However, as quaint as those places were, I was at a point in my trip after driving for two days when I just wanted to get to my final destination. Taking the scenic route delayed that and caused me some frustration along the way when I'd get behind drivers who were of a different mind than me. On the next two trips to Maine, I stayed on 95 North as far as I could go before turning off and heading east toward the island. So consider when you want to "just get there" and when you have time for sightseeing along the way before you make that wrong turn.

5. *Touchstones from Home.* Take some "toys" with you from home that you can use during your free times. If you like to draw or paint, pack a sketch pad and some pencils or some canvasses and your paint kit. Chances are, you'll be taking a camera. But if you're a photography buff, include those extra lenses, filters, disks or rolls of film for capturing the unique aspects of your vacation spot. A deck of cards, a good book, crossword puzzles, a kite—I'm sure you can think of lots more of these items to take along to make your trip enjoyable.

Traveling by yourself dot com

Traveling by yourself does not mean you have to be alone the entire time. Heavens, that could get old really fast! The type of trip you take can be centered around meeting other solo travelers and sharing your adventures together. I recently googled—Isn't it amazing all the new verbs in our vocabulary since the Internet?—the words 'solo traveler' and came up with an incredible array of websites and blogs devoted to people traveling on their own. And, while I've never used these sites myself and am not recommending any one in particular, here are a few that piqued my interest enough that I may try them out in the future.

- www.independenttraveler.com
- www.solotraveller.com
- www.women-traveling.com
- www.solotravelerblog.com

In summary, I want to share with you what that first trip to Maine meant to me. I mentioned that I'd asked for a secluded place where I could write and read. That trip was purposely planned to be introspective for me. It was taken at a time when I was re-evaluating my life's choices and wanted to think about what to do next. I had just finished reading James Redfield's "The Celestine Prophecy," and had purchased the supplemental "The Experiential Guide." My intent was to complete the guide and see where it took me spiritually. I also wanted to write some essays and poems as part of this process.

I am happy to report that I was successful in fulfilling my intentions and came away with a lot more than I'd gone there seeking. I found myself laughing and crying and feeling and learning and just plain enjoying my own company! It was a very pivotal journey for me, and I recommend that you consider taking a journey of this type at some point in your life. You deserve it!

Chapter Eight - Recommendations

1. It's self-talk time again. I think you'll find that your "conversations" with yourself when planning this longer vacation alone will go to deeper levels. You may come up with more excuses why *not* to do this—and perhaps they'll be legitimate. This step will require you to be ready and willing in ways that the other steps did not. Allow yourself the time you need to think and "talk" about it before going where you're not ready. At the same time, don't keep putting it off if in your heart of hearts you know you should, and can, do this.

2. Because this trip may require more time and dollars, plan accordingly and begin the process early. Allow time for postal requests to be delivered and for recipients to respond to your inquiries. Begin a budget where you can save a little every pay that will help alleviate the cost of this trip. If you're going to a popular location or during a busy time, you'll want to get your reservations in early enough. The same goes for plane reservations—the best deals often require at least three to four weeks lead time. In other words, timing is everything.

3. Packing—the same rule applies as it did in chapter seven: Keep it light! If you're driving your own vehicle, you'll have the advantage of being able to bring a lot more than if you're flying or otherwise. But you should still keep it to a minimum. Remember, you'll have to lug all that stuff into your room or cabin once you arrive!

4. So I'm not redundant here, you can refer to recommendations given in previous chapters. This is not a new experience, just a longer one.

5. When you're home again, don't forget to congratulate yourself! As a matter of fact, you can do that as you're planning the vacation and any time during it when you feel the need to reassure yourself that you're okay, or when you're feeling really good about where you are and what you're doing! Good job!

Suggestions

Obviously, any book that meets your criteria for a "good read" should be included on your list of "things to take along." Here are some to consider.

1. Any "Harry Potter" book by J.K. Rowling. Talk about letting the imagination run wild! What a great, fun companion for a vacation on your own!

2. "The Hobbit" and "The Lord of the Rings" trilogy by J.R.R. Tolkien. "The Hobbit" was first published in 1937, but continues to be a best seller over 70 years later. These delightful fantasy books are wonderful for a long getaway when you can let your imagination soar to the Middle Earth and back. (Even if you've seen the movies!)

3. Any Nelson DeMille book. I particularly like the ones with the character John Corey, ex-NYPD detective, but I have never been disappointed in any of his novels.

4. The early "Kay Scarpetta" books by Patricia Cornwell. Join the Chief Medical Examiner of Virginia as she and her cohorts solve some gruesome crimes. While the details may sometimes be gritty, you're sure to be riveted to your seat as you play amateur sleuth and try to solve the crime yourself before the last page reveals all.

CHAPTER NINE

THE EXTENDED HOLIDAY

I 'll be the first to admit that taking an extended trip alone, say for three, four or more weeks, is not for everyone. A vacation of that length requires a real desire to *be* wherever it is you want to go, regardless of the fact that you may have to go it alone. That's how it happened for me. I didn't set out thinking *Where can I go on a month-long vacation alone?* It was the other way around. I had a desire to go to Great Britain, then started the process of planning it.

It all began when I was driving home to New York in September of '82 after meeting my family in Nags Head, North Carolina, for a week's vacation. Driving along Interstate 95 north through Delaware and New Jersey, I reminisced about the week past and about my trip to Colorado earlier that year. *Where to next year?* I wondered. *How about Great Britain?* was my inner voice's reply. I'd always been drawn to Great Britain, especially Scotland and northern England, whether through romance and mystery novels, history books, movies or music. *Okay,* I thought, *who will I get to go with me? Diane? Gail?* (See, even *I* don't always plan to do things all by myself. I like companions as much as the next person!) By the time I arrived home, I had pretty much decided that I would spend two weeks of my vacation in 1983 in Great Britain, hopefully with a friend but possibly on my own.

As it turned out, I decided to defer my remaining week of vacation in '82 to the following year and take a full month in Great Britain in September. That gave me time to save up money for the trip and make arrangements for places to stay and events to attend. Of course, none of my friends were able to take that amount of time off or were interested in going to Great Britain, even to meet me for a week's time. But I was so psyched by then that I was actually going to my dream destination, I didn't care about going solo!

The arrangements

Planning a trip of this magnitude alone is both the *same* as when planning an overnighter or a week-long trip and *different*. It's the same in that you have to decide the best time to go, what you want to do while there, what to pack, where to stay and all the rest of those logistics related to traveling. You can refer back to the previous chapters, and your own traveling experiences, to know what's involved. If you're going out of the country, remember to check into passports, immunization requirements and other conditions associated with international travel. You'll probably want to give yourself more time for the planning process as well.

What's different, in my opinion, is how you approach it psychologically and emotionally. A month alone on a trip is a scary thought. *What if I don't like it, but I'm stuck there for the duration of the trip? How dangerous will it be for me? Can I really spend that much time alone without getting bored or going crazy?* And if your trip takes you out of the country, that creates even more concerns. *I'll be so far from home! The customs are so different. The people are so different. Will there be a language barrier?*

What will happen if this or that occurs? Believe me, all these thoughts went through my mind as I prepared for my trip to Great Britain. But I wasn't to be deterred.

Allow yourself to feel all the anxieties and doubts associated with planning a long-term trip like this. Allow yourself to feel the excitement and anticipation as well. Then, weigh your *pros* and *cons* and make your decision. Maybe you'll decide that it's not the time or the vacation for you. That's okay—at least you gave it a chance! But maybe you'll decide it is—wow!!!

The journey is not the adventure...
The destination is not the adventure...
Life is the adventure!

This quote says to me that we need to recognize the adventure that exists in the *process of preparing* for a journey such as this, not just in the journey itself. The year it took me to plan my British holiday is as much a part of the memory of that trip as the trip itself. The early months were spent *gathering*—information, money, clothes, ideas. I got books from the library and book stores–travel guides and books about inns, castles and other interesting places to stay and visit. I kept a "wish list" of things that came to mind to do or see, simply writing them down, to be organized at a later date when I started working out the details of the trip. I taught some classes in tarot card reading to make extra spending money. I wrote—and rewrote—lists of things to pack, going through my closet and deciding what I had and what I needed to buy. I checked into requirements for traveling out of the country, discovering I only needed a passport for Great Britain. No shots!

Then, one morning in January of '83, I awoke to find myself snowbound at home, not able to drive down the hills on which I lived to go to work in Greenwich, Connecticut. *Darn! Guess I'll just have to find some way to amuse myself!* So, all day long, I huddled over my kitchen table, books and maps and lists spread out all around me as I plotted out my journey. I'd made an enlarged copy of a map of the island, and I marked on it the places I absolutely wanted to visit. They included: Edinburgh (International Art Festival); Balmoral (Royal Highland Games); Hawthorne (Home of the Brontë sisters and locale for *Wuthering Heights*); Stratford-upon-Avon (Royal Shakespeare Theatre); Stonehenge; Cornwall and Rye (havens for smugglers and pirates); and, of course, London. Then, I connected the dots! After studying the results, I decided that I'd start my journey in Glasgow, Scotland, and end it in London.

The next step was to make up the itinerary and write letters to the various inns and hotels where I'd stay. I also had to book airline reservations, purchase tickets to Shakespeare plays, order a discount pass for visiting tourist sites, arrange for a rental car—you get the picture!

Romantic interlude

I'm not going to get into the details here about my trip—that could be another book! But I did promise you earlier that I'd tell you about meeting Stuart, so I will. As I explained in chapter four, Stuart and I met in the Blithe Spirit pub in Edinburgh my second day in Great Britain. We chatted for a while over my dinner, then we went to another pub down the street called The Rose Pub. We had a nice visit over a beer and exchanged addresses, then I headed for the Military Tattoo at the castle.

The next morning I was going to drive into the highlands to Balmoral to attend the Royal Highland Games. When I went to the dining room of my hotel for breakfast, there was a beautiful pinkish-yellow rose in a juice glass at my assigned table. And under the glass was a note written on the back of a darts score sheet from the hotel's bar. The note and the rose were from Stuart—he'd left them at the front desk the evening before, and the staff was kind enough to put them on my breakfast table. The note, written in a humorous yet sincere tone, said that he'd had a good time the night before, he wished he'd thought to invite me for drinks after the Tattoo, he'd like to get postcards from me as I traveled through Great Britain and that I should have a good time at the highland games. What a nice surprise and pleasant beginning to the day!

So, I sent him a couple of postcards as I traveled south into England. About ten days later, when I arrived at my hotel in Stratford-upon-Avon, there was a single red rose and a letter waiting for me when I checked in. A week later in Devon, another rose awaited me on my arrival at my inn, and Stuart called to ask if I would I like to see him when he was—*coincidentally? I think not!*—in London on business the same days I'd be there? I was excited for two reasons—the obvious one and because I was craving some companionship by this time.

We met in London at the Dr. Watson Bar in the Sherlock Holmes Hotel (Could I make that up?) and Stuart brought—you guessed it!—a single red rose for me. Over the next three days, we went rowing on Serpentine Lake in Hyde Park, toured the Tower of London and shared romantic dinners and walks along the Thames River. By the time he took me to Heathrow Airport for my return flight to New York, I was "in love!"

Long story short, we courted over the phone and via the postal service for ten months; he visited me in July of '84; proposed to me when I took him to Newark Airport; and we were married on November 24, 1984! Quite a whirlwind romance, wasn't it? And the fact that the marriage ended less than four years later does not *in the least* take away from those special, romantic memories!

Chicken or egg?

As in the popular query, *What came first: the chicken or the egg?*, taking an extended vacation becomes a question of what came first— your desire to be in a particular place or your desire to be away for a particular length of time? Usually, as in my case, it's the first desire and, if that place is far enough away from home, staying for a longer period of time makes sense. First of all, you'll want to get your money's worth for the cost of getting there. Why spend hundreds, perhaps thousands, of dollars on airfare only to turnaround in one week and return home? Along that same thought, you don't want to adjust to the time zone change and jet lag only to find yourself shifting gears again to go home. It's not healthy. Once at your destination, you don't want the visit to be a blur of activities, rushing from one place to another, trying to see and do as much within the limited time as possible. How many times have you come back from a vacation more stressed out than you were when you left, feeling the need for a vacation from your vacation?

Instead, the extended vacation should allow you to take your time and get to know the people and place you are visiting, whether you spend the trip driving from locale to locale as I did or stay in one place the entire time. It gives you room to breathe and to get to know yourself better, too. Ah, there's the rub! Maybe that's the scariest thought about all of this for you—getting to know yourself better.

Is it wrong to feel this way? No, not wrong, just unnecessary. The unknown is often scary, but that doesn't mean that it's inaccessible or unfriendly. It wasn't always easy for me, driving around Great Britain alone, spending a day here or three days there, meeting people but not having a companion. In fact, about two-thirds of the way through the trip, I was miserably lonely and bored. I was in an area of the country that I didn't find particularly interesting, but I had to go through it to get to Devon. I wished desperately that someone was with me, and I even thought about cutting the trip short, heading directly to London and then on home.

How did I deal with this dilemma? First, I allowed myself to shed a few tears and wallow in my loneliness for a while. Nothing like a little self-pity to make one feel better for a while, then even lonelier! Once I'd sniffled my last sniff, I started thinking about the state I was in and came to realize something important. Those bouts of loneliness and boredom can just as easily happen at home as away from it. Those feelings of being "alone in a crowded room" can come over you any time, unannounced. So, the question became, do I succumb to this momentary bout and prematurely cut short a lifelong dream or do I get back in the car and proceed as planned? Well, I'm pleased to say that I chose the latter option and am so glad that I did!

Chapter Nine - Recommendations

1. If there was ever a time for self-talk, this is it. As in the previous chapters, get in touch with your feelings about the possibility of making a trip of this kind. Listen to your body as it reacts to those feelings. Listen to your soul as it speaks to you of deeper reasons why you should or shouldn't proceed.

2. If you decide that an extended holiday alone is not for you, at least not at this time in your life, don't lament it. Give yourself credit for going through the discerning process and being honest with yourself. Remember what I stated at the beginning of this chapter—it's not for everyone.

3. Whether going on this trip or not, there *is* a place you can visit any time for as long as you desire. It's a place called *Imaginenation*. It's a delightful place where whimsy is the *modus operandi* and "Go for it!" is the only law.

    Select a place you'd love to visit. Then, go to the library, bookstore and Internet and gather as much information about this place as you can. Read about it. Take a class and learn the language. Try some recipes for dishes for which this location is known. Listen to music that originates in this locale. Throw a party with your special place as the theme. Come up with your own ways to "visit" this place that are fun for you. Sit in the quiet of your room, close your eyes and see yourself there—walking the streets, conversing with the natives, eating the food—you get the idea! Who knows? Maybe you'll even be inspired to go there in person someday—alone or otherwise!

4. Are you actually going to do it? Are you seriously going to take an extended holiday alone? Congratulations! The same suggestions given in earlier chapters apply here, as do the ones I mentioned in this chapter. Yes, you'll probably need more clothes than on shorter trips, but packing lightly is still of prime importance. Besides, you'll want room to bring back all those new clothes and souvenirs you'll be buying while traveling!

If going out of the country, learn about the money and exchange rate for the currency. An electrical adapter kit might come in handy for your hair appliances or razor. One of those English translation books probably won't hurt if your destination is not a predominantly English-speaking country. Don't forget a passport and check into any special rules regarding travel in the areas you'll visit, as well as the laws about driving.

5. Welcome home! I hope your experience was as rewarding and memorable as mine. Now, put all those photographs, ticket stubs, playbills and other mementos in a photo album/scrap book. Share it with your friends and, whenever you get the urge, you can take that journey again and again through your mind's eye!

CHAPTER TEN

MAKING ROOM FOR LIFE

A s I mentioned in chapter five, I arrived at Park City, Utah, in September of 2000. I came for a two-day visit and, as of 2012, haven't left yet. This visit was part of a solitary journey unlike any other for me, a journey that began in September of '98. That's when I got this idea from somewhere deep in my soul to sell my house and things, quit my job and head west. It took two years to bring to fruition, but I finally sold my house and most of my possessions in August 2000, put the rest of my things in storage, packed up my new Jeep Cherokee Sport and hit the road.

If you haven't figured it out by now, I have a passion for driving long distances. I love setting out on the highways and byways, sometimes with no destination in mind as I explore new territories, then study the map to see where I've *been*, not where I'm going. Luckily, I'm blessed with a navigational mind that makes it easy for me to find my way around. I attribute this wanderlust to two things. The first is my heritage. I'm half Hungarian, so I'm sure that there's gypsy blood flowing through my veins, blood that sets my nomadic urges on edge until I have to get behind the wheel and venture forth.

The second reason can be traced back to summer vacations as a child—I managed to finagle my way on my maternal grandparents' trip each year. We put miles and miles on the odometer as we drove through Ohio, Pennsylvania, Maryland, Virginia, Tennessee, Arkansas and Kentucky. We visited Civil War sites, explored underground caves, toured horse ranches and stopped at those unusual attractions advertised on billboards and barns, like reptile farms and gravity-defying houses.

I'd sit in the back seat of Grandpa Todd's Cadillac, studying the triple-A maps and observing every road sign and milepost. There was this one incident when we wanted to go somewhere—the place escapes me—and Grandpa turned left at the crossroads. I, in my precocious nine-year old way, said, "No, Grandpa, we want to go *that* way," pointing to the right. He just chuckled, even when my Grandma Rose suggested that maybe he should pay attention to me, until he realized that we were headed in the wrong direction! Needless to say, he wasn't too happy about having to do an about-face as Grandma and I chuckled.

Getting back to my journey west, while I won't go into the details here, I will tell you that I experienced incredible highs, depressing lows, but mostly a lot of pleasant in-betweens. I was apprehensive, elated, nervous, confident, happy, sad, energetic, bored, impressed, overwhelmed, sad, zealous—my emotions ran the gamut from A to Z. There was even a stretch, just before I reached Utah, when I was really missing my nieces and nephew back in Ohio so much that I thought about turning around and going home. I'm so glad I got over that hump or I wouldn't be where I am today—and there's a good chance you wouldn't have this book to read now!

Parked in Park City

Four weeks after departing Ohio, having traveled to Chicago, Milwaukee, Minneapolis, South Dakota, Montana and Wyoming, I arrived in Salt Lake City, where I spent two days getting utilitarian things done—oil changed, photos developed, prescription filled, e-mail checked, clothes laundered. I then headed back east into the mountains to spend two days in Park City, because I was considering returning in January to volunteer for Robert Redford's Sundance Film Festival and I wanted to check it out.

As soon as I drove into town, I knew I'd have to extend my stay at least another two days. From talking to residents that first afternoon, I discovered that this place is like a "Twilight Zone"—people come to visit and never leave! Within a few hours, I decided to give myself a week to find a job and a place to live for the winter or I would continue on, heading south to Arizona and New Mexico. You see, I'd always wondered what it would be like to spend a winter and Christmas in the mountains. I'd also thought it would be fun to live in a resort town as a local instead of a tourist. Plus, if I lived here, I wouldn't have to travel back in January for the festival. Well, it only took two days to get a job—as the administrative assistant to the director of Skier Services and his staff at Deer Valley Resort—and to find a room to rent.

What a winter! I made a lot of wonderful friends, learned to ski again and took a writing class that prompted me to take this book off the shelf and finish it. When spring rolled around, everyone told me, "If you like it here in the winter, you've got to see it in the summer—you'll love it!" So I decided to see for myself…and I haven't left yet! I truly fit the saying we have here, "You come for the winters and stay for the summers."

Another one of my passions is hiking. Ever since my days trekking through the Superstition Mountains in Arizona, I've enjoyed traversing mountains, walking trails through woods and along streambeds and climbing over rocky terrain. You can imagine my joy when I discovered that miles and miles of trails have been laid out throughout the mountains in and around Park City. So, I picked up a map at the Chamber of Commerce and began exploring. While I do go hiking with friends, as with any alone activity, they aren't always available or interested when I am, so I venture out on my own.

Hiking offers me many rewards. There are the obvious physical benefits of walking, climbing and being outdoors, especially in this pure mountain atmosphere. Mentally, I'm able to clear away the cobwebs and think through concerns that need resolving or come up with some creative ideas to pursue. But it's the benefit to my spirit that I value the most.

Hiking in these mountains is a sensual experience, if you allow yourself to be aware and alert to your surroundings. Feeling the solid earth beneath my hiking boots...seeing the multitude of multi-hued wild flowers that adorn the trails and the expansive blue sky...smelling the pine trees and the foliage...hearing the harmony of birds and streams and wind...tasting the crisp mountain air. My spirit is refreshed after an invigorating hike, and the rest of me is uplifted by this enlivened spirit.

My life here in Park City is itself fodder for another book. I'm still working at Deer Valley Resort, where I am now a full-time, year-round employee. I served for four years on the Board of Trustees of the Unity Spiritual Center, where I also led guided meditations, occasionally filled in for the minister in her absence and recorded a CD of guided mediations with a local musician. I also served for two years on the Park City Film Series board. I performed with a local comedy troupe called *Off the Top*. In fact, after a four-week class in improvisational comedy, I was one of the initial founders of the troupe—who'd have thought a non-credit class could lead to such a wild and lucrative venture? During the summer of 2005, I conducted a 13-week workshop based on the book, "The Artist's Way," that was so successful, I repeated it in the winters of 2006 and 2007. I was also the publicity chair and silent auction chair for the American Cancer Society's Relay For Life for three years.

So, it's plain to see that my two-day stop in Park City, Utah, has certainly proven to be an incredible, invaluable experience that is still unfolding. I share all this with you so you'll see that self-discovery from time spent in your own company doesn't end. It's an ongoing process. What's important is that you take control of this process, direct your own course and make your own decisions as to what you experience.

Chapter Ten - Recommendations

Don't worry—I'm not going to suggest that you sell everything and hit the road! What I am going to suggest, however, is that you think about what would be involved if you *were* to make such an extraordinary decision.

1. How attached are you to your "things?" Would you be able to let go of them if it became necessary? When was the last time you cleaned out the clutter in your house—I mean, really cleaned it out? Do this, even if only on paper. What's easy to get rid of and why? What would you have difficulty parting with and why? Are there things that you keep out of fear that someday you'll need them? A good gauge is "If you haven't used it or worn it in a year, get rid of it!"

2. Now, get rid of *something* today, no matter how small, something that you've been keeping for forever but which you have absolutely no use for. Donate it to a charity, give it to a friend or family member, throw it away—whatever! The idea is to "let go" of this thing that has such a strong hold on you. Once you've got rid of one thing, do another, then another. Trust me, it feels great to actually clean out the clutter!

3. Your ability to let go of "things"—or your need to hoard them— says a lot about how you hold onto feelings and thoughts as well. Are there feelings you are harboring, feelings that have been around for a long time but serve no real purpose today? Do you have difficulty letting go of these feelings for fear of not having any to replace them? Is your mind cluttered with thoughts about people or events that caused you pain in the

past? Do some real soul searching here and clean out your cluttered mind and soul. Consider seeking professional assistance in the form of a life coach, counselor or therapist. It won't be a quick or easy process, but it will definitely be beneficial to lightening up your spirit.

4. If you *were* to make such a drastic change in your life, what form would it take? Would you quit your job and go to school? Or maybe start your own business? Would you sell your house and move to a smaller, simpler place? Would you travel? Even if you have a family to consider or someone else will be involved in the final decision, this kind of assessment requires solitary thoughts and feelings before you make your contribution to that final decision.

5. What if you decide that the way your life is right now is the way you want it to be? That there's nothing you would change? Well, what's wrong with that? That's a good thing to know and acknowledge—and I'll bet it makes you feel good, too! Just remember to repeat this analysis of your life every now and then so you can clean out the clutter, both literally and figuratively.

Suggestions

These books offer thought-provoking and inspiring exercises that will assist you in "cleaning out the clutter" of your life.

1. "Artist's Way: A Spiritual Path to Higher Creativity." 1995. Julia Cameron. Putnam Publishing Group. New York, New York.

2. "What Color is Your Parachute?" Published annually. Richard Nelson Bolles. Ten Speed Press. Berkeley, California.

3. "The Experiential Guide" to the book, "The Celestine Prophecy." 1994. James Redfield. Warner Books, Inc. New York, New York

CHAPTER ELEVEN

TENDING YOUR GARDEN

In the opening paragraph of chapter one, I stated that "...my time with others is enhanced by my time alone." Leonardo da Vinci told you in chapter seven to "...go away, have a little relaxation..."; and, Dr. Wayne Dyer explained how balance is necessary to achieve proper perspective in our lives. Spending time alone is an integral element to achieving that balance.

What follows is an essay that I wrote for an English composition class in 1992. It's a study of Jerzy Kosinski's book, "Being There," and the subsequent movie of the same name, and I believe it will help explain the value of creating alone time in our lives.

* * * * *

Chance pushed his way...toward the exit...Chance was bewildered. He reflected and saw the withered image of Chauncey Gardiner: it was cut by the stroke of a stick through a stagnant pool of rain water. His own image was gone as well...

Chance pushed the heavy glass door open and stepped out into the garden...The garden lay calm, still sunk in repose...Not a thought lifted itself from Chance's brain. Peace filled his chest.

(Kosinski 117-8)

Even though I saw the movie version years ago starring Peter Sellers, I only recently read Kosinski's book, "Being There." I was moved by the way Kosinski dealt with the complexity of the human psyche in such a simple story and was even more amazed at how well the story has withstood the passage of time. When published, we were in the midst of a controversial war and social "revolution"—the ramifications of which have infiltrated the very fiber of our existence ever since. Yet, Kosinski's message is timeless, having as much value and significance today as it did then, maybe even more so. I feel compelled to express my thoughts on this tale and share them with whomever feels compelled to pay them heed.

Kosinski's Chance, the main character in his novel, is a man who has spent his entire life in seclusion. For forty years, Chance's life centers around two things—watching television and tending his garden—and he successfully manages to maintain a balance between these two aspects of his life. He is content. When circumstances force him to leave his home and he is faced with new experiences or relationships, he draws upon the knowledge he has gleaned over the years watching television, transfers it to the immediate situation and acts accordingly. It doesn't occur to him to do otherwise. It doesn't occur to him that he is, as the reader sees him, a "fish out of water."

On the surface, his encounters are comical and whimsical, bringing a chuckle to the readers' lips at the incredulity of the situations. But in the five short days that transpire, there is a change going on deep inside of Chance. The passage quoted above, which is the last in the book, suggests the first signs of his confusion and frustration. What he doesn't realize is that his life is out of balance. For the last five days, he's only been living one aspect of the life he had known for the past forty years—watching television. What's been missing is his gardening.

The book, and subsequently the film version, satirically plays up the humor of Chance's obsession with television. When Chance does talk about gardening, the metaphors are looked upon by the reader as amusing evidence that he lacks a grasp of reality. I believe, however, that the message Kosinski is conveying goes even deeper than the interactions and reactions of Chance's experiences. It's about balance in our lives—what it is, what happens when we shift off it and how we can get it back.

It is my premise that in "Being There," watching television symbolizes the external elements of life and the garden, the internal. When Chance goes for days without tending his garden, he is denied the peace and tranquility that balance the activity of his life. He's off kilter. While he may not be aware of *why* he's feeling the way he is, as the book comes to an end he is drawn to the garden as a place of security and peace. Even in the final scene of the film, while attending Rand's funeral, Chance is attracted to the nearby woods. He wanders off alone, reveling in nature's splendor, obviously happy in the world he has missed.

Acknowledgement

The film also offers a scene not in the book, a scene that first opened my eyes to the depths of Chance's soul and the possible intent of Kosinski's story. It is when the doctor confronts Chance at Rand's deathbed, saying he really *is* just Chance and he really *is* just a gardener after all. For the first time, Chance expresses emotion and gets tears in his eyes as he affirms what he has known all along, but for which he had never been acknowledged—the simple truth of who he is. Isn't that what we all want, to be acknowledged for who we are?

Yet, all too often, we look outside ourselves for that acknowledgement. We search for external goals and stimulations, external rela-

119

tionships and feedback, to direct our attention. We are so engrossed in this search that when external elements are lacking, our thoughts and actions become chaotic and we experience inner disorder. When left alone, we begin to wonder about things. And unless we have control over our consciousness, our wondering turns to worrying, about health, jobs, relationships, finances—whatever potential problems we can imagine. So we search for diversions.

Television plays an important part in diverting our attention. Although the experience of watching television may generally leave people feeling passive, weak and even irritable, the predictability and redundancy of the shows and commercials keep unpleasant concerns or personal worries out of our minds. TV is turned on for companionship, as soon as we awake or return home. The same is true of the stereo or the car radio. How many people could drive for seven hours without turning on the radio or popping in a cassette? It's as if we need constant distractions from—what? Ourselves? Being alone? Just what is it we fear about being alone? About talking to ourselves? Or, more importantly, about listening to ourselves? How can we sustain balance in our lives unless we allow ourselves time to be alone, time to tend our 'gardens?'

Actually, there are times when we tend our 'gardens' without being aware of doing so. If you've ever been so immersed in a project or book or craft that you've completely lost track of time and your surroundings, you've been in your 'garden.' If you've ever participated in a sport, like running or swimming or skiing, and felt everything "come together"—mind and body working in perfect harmony—you've been in your 'garden.' In his book, "Flow: The Psychology of Optimal Experience," Mihaly Csikszentmihalyi calls these experiences 'flow,' and goes on to explain how we must develop the ability to find enjoyment and purpose regardless of external circumstances.

For me, driving alone for miles and hours can be a 'flow' experience. Some may argue that we can achieve 'flow' by being engrossed for hours in a television show. But Csikszentmihalyi disagrees, contending "...one expends a great deal of attention [watching television] without having much to show for it afterward," unlike the experiences described above.

Daydream believer

Another way to tend our 'gardens' is to daydream. Remember when we were children and we were encouraged to use our imaginations? Remember daydreaming about being a prima ballerina or a famous ball player or an Olympic gold medal winner? The joy of daydreaming need not be confined to childhood. Take the time to sit in your easy chair, with no television or music playing in the background, and let your mind wander where it will. For some, this is actually a scary thought, which is all the more reason to try it. Just relax. The birds chirping outside the window or the drone of the neighbor's lawnmower or the ticking of your clock are not distractions, but act as lullabies to help your mind drift off...let it create something wonderful for you. Don't be limited by *can'ts* or *shouldn'ts*. If you're a writer, see yourself autographing copies of your latest novel at a bookstore. An engineer? See that magnificent building you designed reaching to the heavens. Whatever you aspire to, feel the moment—the pride, the excitement, the glee—as your mind takes you on this incredible journey. And know that these thoughts are flowers you are gathering from your garden, the beauty and scent of which will motivate and comfort you when you revert back to the external world.

Similar to daydreaming is a third method of visiting our 'gardens'— meditation. Ever since the Maharishi Mahesh Yogi introduced Transcendental Meditation to the United States in the mid-70s, more and more people are turning to some form of meditation to create the balance so necessary in their lives. There are no mystical, magical secrets or rituals to meditating. The mantras of TM and the positions of yoga are only techniques for personal preference and variation. All that's required to meditate is to sit in a quiet environment with eyes closed and body relaxed, breathing deeply and evenly and letting go of all conscious thoughts by gently focusing on one word, sound or thought.

The experience is not unlike immersing in an ocean. Imagine your external, physical, conscious self as the surface of the ocean, sometimes calm and sometimes turbulent, but always moving. As you meditate, you travel down through the depths of the ocean to where the waters are calmer and the atmosphere tranquil. Eventually, you reach the ocean bed—your subconscious mind, your inner 'garden'—and the activities of the surface are far away and forgotten.

It is from here that balance is attained between our external and internal natures. It is from this perspective in our psyche that our more complex 'self' grows, a self that is able to blend its distinction and its uniqueness with ideas and beings beyond it. It is in the solitude of the 'garden' that we recognize the beauty of the Universe. For it is at this level in the ocean where the surface activity begins—first as a ripple, then a current, until as a wave it crests and crashes on a distant shore. So, too, do our thoughts and ideas begin, at some distant place in our subconscious. And once we have achieved balance and growth, we resurface to integrate the subtle yet powerful experience into our daily lives.

This internal 'garden' I have been referring to is known by many different names—subconscious, soul, inner child, creative mind, divine life, higher self—whatever we chose to call it, it's the center of our being, the place from which come all our ideas and feelings.

Now, I'm not talking about a religious belief here. Religion is an *external* faction, created and controlled by people for the purpose of sharing common beliefs. What I'm referring to is our metaphysical essence, that central part of us that is connected to the Force that governs the Universe. It is Yin to the Yang, passive to the active, spiritual to the corporeal.

We have an abundance of external stimulation and activities available to us. Our society emphasizes and thrives on them, and that's not necessarily bad. What *is* detrimental to our well-being as a people is when we shun the complementary activities that would allow us to maintain the balance we so desperately need. Chance recognized this. While we can't help but be amused by his antics as the mysterious, comical hero of "Being There," we have a hard time relating to him or feeling comfortable with the idea of someone like him. Yet Chance, in his own naïve way, has the secret to leading a happy, balanced life. He knows himself better than most people could admit to and he can teach us a lot. Perhaps a visit with him to our inner 'garden' would be just the remedy we need to relieve ourselves of the fear we have of being alone.

Chapter Eleven - Recommendations

1. Daydreams! Do you remember some of the daydreams you had as a child? Have any of them come true? Do you still have them? Allow yourself the luxury of daydreaming. Create a scenario and see it through, from beginning to end. Feel the joy that comes from believing that *anything* is possible. Now, ask yourself if what you're daydreaming *could* come true and what would you have to do to make it happen. The rest is up to you.

2. "Flow" moments. Have you experienced them? Have you been so engrossed in a project or activity that it seems time has stopped and the world around you has disappeared? Those are valuable moments. Are you allowing yourself the opportunities to get involved in those activities often enough? Be sure to do so in order to be in the "flow" and create balance in your life.

3. If you already know how to meditate, are you doing it often? It's easy to get out of the habit, to have something else to do instead. Make sure you set time aside to meditate each day and say "hello" to your soul as often as possible. If you have never meditated, give it a try. There are many books, tapes and teachers that can guide you through any number of methods of meditating. Explore them and find one that's most comfortable and beneficial for you.

   But even without formal instruction, you can meditate. Simply sit in a quiet place where you won't be disturbed for about 20 minutes. Put both feet on the floor and your hands in your lap or at your sides. Let your body relax—shoulders down and mouth slightly open as your jaw slackens. Close your eyes and take a deep breath through your nose, expanding from your stomach and diaphragm first, then your lungs. Hold the breath comfortably for a few seconds, then slowly exhale through your lips. Feel your whole body going limp as you repeat this slow, peaceful breathing. Let your mind go to a special place, a place where you feel tranquil and safe. Perhaps on a mountaintop, next to a babbling brook, by the ocean or on a porch swing. It's *your* special place where you can return whenever you want. As thoughts of your outside world come into your mind, gently tell them "goodbye...I'll deal with you later," and let them float away as you continue to relax. Listen with your inner ear for your inner voice, which may or may not "talk" to you during the meditation. Simply relax and enjoy!

4. Learn a new activity in which you use your entire being—body, mind and spirit—to achieve your objective. Tai Chi, for instance, is a perfect example. It requires physical discipline, mindful concentration and a harmonious spirit.

5. While this may sound contrary to what we've been talking about in this book—being alone—share your experiences with others. Don't shut them out, creating a vacuum around yourself in your efforts to be comfortable being alone. Remember, it's all about balance, not seclusion.

Suggestions

1. "Being There" by Jerzy Kosinski. A man grows up virtually all alone in a house, knowing only two worlds: television and his garden. Circumstances force him into the real world where, equipped only with these two points of reference, he man-

ages to unwittingly have a tremendous effect on the people he encounters and on the country.

2. "Flow: The Psychology of Optimal Experience" by Mihaly Csikszentmihalyi

3. Any books on meditation, yoga and deep breathing techniques.

EPILOG

How difficult is it for you to spend time alone *now?* Hopefully, your answer is that it's easier than it was when you started reading this book. There are a few points I'd like to make that summarize what I've tried to convey to you on these pages.

First, you should realize that *everyone* harbors some anxieties about doing something, going somewhere or just plain being alone. These anxieties manifest themselves differently from person to person. What bothers you may be easy for another person to do, while that which is simple for you is a major roadblock for the next person. Recognizing and acknowledging your concerns and discomforts about being on your own, and then being willing to do something to overcome them, are valuable lessons to learn.

Second, understand that there's more than one way to be in your own company. Not everything is right for everybody, and you don't have to experience it all. For instance, if you don't like going to the movies *period,* going alone isn't going to prove anything. You will find your niche at your own pace, and you should remember to respect others who are searching for their niche as well.

Third, you'll see and feel improvements in yourself as you perform the exercises in self-discovery and begin spending more time in your own company. The benefits are of a physical, mental, emotional or spiritual nature—or a combination of any or all of these. Your relationships with your family, friends and associates are enhanced because you bring a more interesting person to the alliance. Your self-esteem and self-confidence are significantly increased. And, most importantly, you are empowered to experience your life to its fullest.

Finally, and this may sound contradictory to everything I've said so far, it's important that you create lasting bonds with the people in your life—family, friends, life partners, co-workers, social acquaintances. In the book, "Younger Next Year for Women" by Chris Crowley and Dr. Henry Lodge that I mentioned in chapter six, we're told about our limbic (emotional) brain, which gives us two advantages over reptiles: it lets us love our young and it lets us work in groups. According to Dr. Lodge, "Because of the limbic way we're made, we are not emotional islands. Simply put, *we complete each other.* In both good and bad ways, to be sure, but we do complete each other, and therefore we cannot make it alone." (Crowley & Lodge 302)

The authors go on to explain how connecting with others is a crucial part of our survival as human beings, and I couldn't agree more. Remember my opening statement in chapter one: *I am not a hermit or a social misfit. I enjoy the company of others and often seek it out...I've discovered that my time with others is enhanced by the time I spend alone.* In other words, we create a balance between our time alone and our time with others, each one enriching the other and enriching our lives.

Alone experiences are not just about *doing* something or *going* somewhere by yourself. They're about *being*—being by yourself, being silent, being in touch with your deepest thoughts, being attuned to your soul's voice. Luxuriate in the silence of alone moments, whether those moments are as short as waiting for a red light to change to green or as long as an eight-hour interstate drive. Silence is, as they say, "golden." Solitude is a destination. It's a place to go to rejuvenate your body, refresh your mind and renew your spirit. I encourage you to spend time in silence and in solitude—you'll be pleasantly and joyfully surprised at the peace and the balance that they'll instill into your life and your relationships.

I hope you'll have fun traveling on your solitary journeys of self-discovery. I'm sure that in no time you'll be waking up each morning, proclaiming confidently, *"Today, I'm going to enjoy the pleasure of my company!"*

DINING SOLO? JOIN THE CROWD
BY ZANNE SCHMALZER
FOR MSN CITY GUIDES, JUNE 2007

Sometimes, particularly after a hard day, I set out to luxuriate at a table for one at a favorite restaurant. Knowing that the dishes will come and go, I look forward to taking my seat, opening a book of short essays and dining in silence.

Ironically, I am not alone. Whatever the reason—the increasing number of single people, the growing army of business travelers—there is an emerging trend toward tables for one. Solo diners across the nation are savoring the pleasures of dining on their own.

These pleasures are as diverse as the "solos" themselves. Without any pressure to be a host or sparkling conversationalist, this option can provide a rare stretch of silence in an otherwise over-stimulating day. Some enjoy the people-watching. Most seize the opportunity to catch up on light reading or note-taking. Dining alone means you can eat what you want, when you want and at whatever pace suits your fancy.

Solos-friendly restaurants are easy to identify. Being greeted warmly by the host or maitre d' is an excellent indication of good things to come. If you walk into a restaurant and the hostess lacks discretion—yelling "table for one," for instance—perhaps you should turn around and leave. Paying appropriate attention to your needs is welcome; pity is not. You can bet you are in a restaurant that values the patronage of single diners if there is ample reading material on hand, a wine-by-the-glass list (or better yet, splits) and preset tables that are neither placed conspicuously nor tucked behind the kitchen door.

Solos have the same seating options as any diner, based on availability. Depending on the restaurant, choices can include the dining counter, the bar, a communal table or the dining room.

Not every restaurant has a dining counter, but those that do have it for a reason: Entertainment. Folks who are willing to dine alone are likely "foodies," and what better way to add value to the overall experience than with a view of the action in the kitchen. A grown-up version of the lunch counter, the dining counter is fast becoming a preferred destination.

More and more restaurants are offering excellent values on their bar or lounge menus, making dining at the bar an excellent choice. Furthermore, because the bar is attended by a bartender, reluctant solos get a built-in companion and, as needed, a therapist.

In recent years, communal tables (sometimes known as the "chef's table") have appeared in lounges and dining rooms across the nation, offering solo diners a bit of clever cover. Seated alongside other parties, their status is hard to confirm. A communal table also can provide the option for conversation with others.

Going it alone in the dining room is not for beginners, but it has its charms—primarily among them, the option to dine completely free from distraction. Despite this delight, some solos feel they stand out, believing that companioned diners are gawking in disbelief as they make their way to table. Be assured there is no reason to feel self-conscious. Your fellow diners (hopefully) are focused on their meal—or better yet, their dining companions.

For more information about solo dining visit SoloDining.com.

APPENDIX B

THE ART OF MOSEYING
BY SUSAN MORRELL

Life in our culture is often one big blur: the streaked image of a photograph taken through the window of a speeding care, lines smudged and colors smeared. We move in high gear, hurry from one place to the next, and cram as much into an hour as is humanly possible—then lament the lack of enough hours in the day. We're a fast-moving, constantly active society. We don't take the time to mosey any more.

"To move along slowly; to amble" only defines the *act* of moseying. If performed properly, moseying is a true *art* that leaves you feeling relaxed physically and exhilarated spiritually. Take an imaginary mosey with me, and you'll see what I mean.

We're standing on a sidewalk in the downtown district of a large city. It's mid-week, and it's high noon. People pour out of office buildings like cereal out of boxes. They dash off in every direction—to the post office, the dry cleaners, the card shop, the dentist, the department store, the travel agent. If they have time, they grab a quick sandwich at the closest deli before returning to their offices for a few more busy hours of work before the evening rush hour. It would be easy to get caught up in their frenzy, easy to be jostled and swept away from our intended course of action, so stay focused.

Before taking your first step, inhale deeply through your nostrils; imagine your body is a balloon filling up with air. Hold it for a moment, then slowly let the air escape through your pursed lips. Try it again, and notice how light you feel. Continue breathing in this relaxed manner as your feet tread lightly and you find your natural gait. Resist the urge to fall into step with the madding crowd, moving instead at a leisurely pace.

Let your hands do what feels most comfortable. Slide them into your coat or pants pockets. Clasp them behind your back. Let them just swing at our sides, conforming to the natural rhythm of your stride.

With your head held high, look ahead of you, not down at your shoes. Observe the faces rushing past. Catch someone's eye, then—don't look away. Hold the other person's glance for one second. Two seconds. A curious thing happens. The muscles in your face shift. The ends of your mouth curl up into a grin. Done often enough, the smiles will infuse you with a wondrous aura of well-being.

Once you've mastered the *act* of moseying, you're ready to refine it to an *art*. This involves heightening your senses, noticing things you disregard in your normal haste. See beyond the obvious. A half-dressed mannequin frozen in an unnatural pose. Faded travel posters and cardboard ocean liners. Graffiti art on a bus-stop bench. A bird's nest in the recesses of an awning. An outdated calendar on a barber shop wall.

Breathe in the street smell. The earthy scent of leather and shoe polish; the stinging odor of hair dyes and permanent solutions; the stench of diesel fumes; the fragrances of floral bouquets—all blending with a smorgasbord of aromas flowing from restaurants, taverns and sidewalk pushcarts.

Tune into the sounds. A street musician plays jazzy notes on his saxophone. Passers-by toss clinking coins into his velvet-lined horn case. Bells toll from high steeples. Engines rev. Horns honk. Drivers curse. Tires screech.

As first, your senses may reel from the barrage of stimulation. This is where the art of moseying comes into play. What distinguishes the *art* from the *act* is an attitude of detached awareness. Take a moment to become aware of a particular scene or sound, to appreciate it and to experience it. Then, release it and proceed to the next one. It's like looking at your surroundings through the lens of a camera. You select a subject, bring it into focus, determine the best composition and snap the picture. When complete, you advance the film and continue on to the next photo opportunity.

So, the next time you go out for lunch in a large city—or to a shopping mall, the local park or even your own neighborhood—treat yourself to a mosey. Shift your mind from 'going somewhere, doing something' to 'just being here and now.' The effects are astounding, and your life will be enhanced in subtle, yet powerful, ways.

APPENDIX C

TIPS FOR THE SOLO TRAVELER

What follows is a list of items that you may or may not need for a trip, depending upon where you're going, how you're getting there, what you'll be doing at your destination and how long you'll be staying there. It is not in any particular order of importance nor is it by any means all-inclusive–I'm sure you can think of more to add. Hopefully, it will prompt you to remember what's important to take and what you can leave behind.

1. Miniature toiletries
2. Extra pairs of prescription glasses; and sunglasses
3. Prescriptions filled and extra if needed
4. A journal
5. In the U.S. - postage stamps, regular and post card
6. Addresses and phone numbers of family and friends
7. Disposable cameras
8. Waist packs—leave behind those cumbersome purses, ladies!
9. Folding tote bags to carry home your purchases

10. Travelers checks

11. First aid kit, including antiseptic and anti-itch creams

12. Passport and/or visas

13. Immunization shots

14. Cell phone; charger; batteries

15. Pillow, towels, blanket

16. Extra oil and windshield wiper fluid

17. Maps; AAA tour books ?

18. Emergency car kit ?

19. Laptop computer and charger

20. Non-perishable food items

21. Beach chair

22. Sunscreen lotion; bug spray

23. Thermal underwear; gloves

24. Collapsible umbrella

25. Books: novels, crossword puzzles, magazines

26. Nook or Kindle and chargers

27. Tickets and passes

28. Miniature tool kit

29. Miniature sewing kit

30. Electrical outlet adapter

31. Foreign currency

32. Sports stuff: golf clubs; ski gear; camping gear; swimming goggles

33. Camera gear; batteries; charger; film

34. Mini flashlight

Be sure to leave your affairs in order back home by doing the following, especially if you'll be gone for a week or longer.

1. Have your mail held at the post office.
2. Set timers for a few lights in your home.
3. Leave your itinerary and important phone numbers with family or close friend.
4. Assign a power of attorney in case of emergencies.
5. Arrange for the care of your pets.
6. Cancel your newspaper delivery until your return.
7. Make arrangements for the payment of any bills due during your absence—utilities, cable, rent, insurance. You can also pay some online while traveling.

Finally, here are a few things to remember while enjoying your vacation.

1. Remember, safety first! If your gut tells you "no," don't go. There's a difference between being cautious out of emotional insecurity and being cautious because of a real survival-instinct fear. Listen to your gut and, when in doubt, abandon the idea and do something else. Your life is more important that proving a point.
2. Bartenders can be your friends. Ask them about places to eat, things to do while in their city, places to go and places to avoid, as well.
3. Avoid chain restaurants that you can frequent back home. Instead, try local food, brews and wines. Get a flavor—figuratively and literally—for the place.
4. Treat yourself to a massage, a manicure or a pedicure—or all three! Try a new hairstyle or let your facial hair grow in. (This last one's for my male audience only please!) In other words, *pamper yourself!*

WORKS CITED

Crowley, Chris and Lodge, Dr. Henry. *Younger Next Year for Women*. New York: Workman Publishing Company, 2004.

Csikszentmihalyi, Mihaly. *Flow: The Psychology of Optimal Experience*. New York: Harper & Row, 1990.

Dyer, Dr. Wayne. *Wisdom of the Ages*. New York: HarperCollins Publisher, Inc., 1998.

Kosinski, Jerzy. *Being There*. Bantam Books: New York, 1970.

Lindbergh, Anne Morrow. *Gift from the Sea*. New York: Vintage Books, A Division of Random House, 1955, 1975.

Newman, Mildred and Berkowitz, Bernard with Owen, Jean. *How to Be Your Own Best Friend*. New York: Ballantine Books, 1971.

Walsch, Neale Donald. *Conversations with God, Book 2*. Charlottesville, VA: Hampton Roads Publishing Co., 1997.

Made in the USA
Charleston, SC
26 January 2013